They slew the giants of southern football in and Miami all fell. Yes, the Seminoles scored points, but it was a consistent, unbreakable matrix of great defensive men who made the great victories of that decade possible and memorable. In "FSU's Sons of the Sixties: A Case for the Defense," Hall of Fame defensive stars John Crowe and Dale McCullers chronicle how FSU's commitment to defense defined the Seminoles' decade of success and helped launch the careers of a Who's Who of college and NFL Head Coaches.

– Charlie Barnes, Author of "Dynasty" and featured columnist in Unconquered magazine

Johnny Crowe and Dale McCullers, former football players at Florida State University have produced a most interesting book. "FSU's Sons of the Sixties: A Case for the Defense" provides readers with an insider's look at the role played by defensive players in the development of a big time college football program. The authors, both of whom have been very successful in their lives after football — one in the corporate world and the other in government service — are positive in their feelings about college football. It is an important and timely publication to be pondered at this time when the future direction to be taken by college football is being debated and discussed. I recommend the book not only to FSU fans but to all readers possessing a genuine interest in the workings of college football.

– Jim Joanos, Retired Judge and author of the numerous articles in the Garnet and Old publication

John Crowe and Dale McCullers — two of the best FSU Hall of Fame members — have done a great job of documenting a wonderful era of Seminole football, the 1960s. Their book, "FSU's Sons of the Sixties: A Case for the Defense," is interesting, entertaining, and a must-read for all Seminole football fans. It is, absolutely, a touchdown: Florida State. Go Noles!

– Gene Deckerhoff, "Voice of the Seminoles"

Two FSU Athletic Hall of Fame recipients, Johnny Crowe and Dale Mc-Cullers, have co-authored a genuinely interesting book about how defensive football played a vital role in establishing a winning tradition at FSU during the decade of the 1960s. I encourage you to get a copy of the book and see for yourself. I found "FSU's Sons of the Sixties: A Case for the Defense" to be superbly written, historically accurate, and downright exciting to read."

– Coach Bobby Bowden, legendary football coach

In their book "FSU's Sons of the Sixties: A Case for the Defense," John Crowe and Dale McCullers have created an exceptional story about a bygone era of Seminole football. Set in the decade of the '60s, the featured FSU defensive players and coaches and their unique stories, seem to come alive to both excite the mind and warm the heart. Well-conceived and superbly written, this book is a treasure of Seminole memories for me personally, and it is a must read for all sports fans who love college football.

– Lee Corso, former player, coach and TV personality
on ESPN's "GameDay" show

FSU'S SONS OF THE SIXTIES

A Case for the Defense

THE SEVEN MAGNIFICENTS
AND THE FORGOTTEN FOUR

JOHN CROWE AND DALE MCCULLERS

FSU'S SONS OF THE SIXTIES: A CASE FOR THE DEFENSE

1405 SW 6th Avenue • Ocala, Florida 34471 • Phone 352-622-1825 • Fax 352-622-1875
Website: www.atlantic-pub.com • Email: sales@atlantic-pub.com
SAN Number: 268-1250

Library of Congress Cataloging-in-Publication Data

Names: Crowe, John B., author. | McCullers, Dale, author.
Title: FSU's sons of the sixties : a case for the defense / by John Crowe and Dale McCullers.
Other titles: Florida State University's sons of the sixties
Description: Ocala, Florida : Atlantic Publishing Group, Inc., 2019. | Includes bibliographical references and index.
Identifiers: LCCN 2018053326 (print) | LCCN 2018061252 (ebook) | ISBN 9781620236253 (ebook) | ISBN 9781620236246 (pbk. : alk. paper) | ISBN 9781620236260 (hardcover : alk. paper) | ISBN 1620236249
Subjects: LCSH: Florida State University—Football—History. | Florida State Seminoles (Football team)—History.
Classification: LCC GV958.F56 (ebook) | LCC GV958.F56 C64 2019 (print) | DDC 796.332/630975988—dc23
LC record available at https://lccn.loc.gov/2018053326

Printed in the United States

PROJECT MANAGER: Danielle Lieneman
INTERIOR LAYOUT AND JACKET DESIGN: Nicole Sturk

Over the years, we have adopted a number of dogs from rescues and shelters. First there was Bear and after he passed, Ginger and Scout. Now, we have Kira, another rescue. They have brought immense joy and love not just into our lives, but into the lives of all who met them.

We want you to know a portion of the profits of this book will be donated in Bear, Ginger and Scout's memory to local animal shelters, parks, conservation organizations, and other individuals and nonprofit organizations in need of assistance.

*– **Douglas & Sherri Brown**,*
President & Vice-President of Atlantic Publishing

TABLE OF CONTENTS

PART 1: BACKGROUND AND THEME

PART 2: COACHES' CORNER

PART 3: SEMINOLE MEMORIES

We dedicate this book in the memory of U.S. Army Lieutenant Johnnie P. Stephens, Jr. — a great teammate and leader of men. Johnnie was killed in action in South Vietnam on April 22, 1969.

The authors intend to have the proceeds and donations from this book go to the Florida State University Unconquered Campaign in the name of Johnnie P. Stephens Jr. for athletic scholarships.

"Greater love has no one than this, than to lay down one's life for one's friends."

John 15:13

EXCERPT FROM "AN AMERICAN HERO... JOHNNIE P. STEPHENS, JR." AS IT APPEARED IN GARNET AND OLD 12/2003

Jim Joanos

Johnnie Perry Stephens, Jr. died as he had lived — a leader of men. Early on the morning of April 22, 1970, U.S. Army Lieutenant Stephens, age 23, was leading his platoon in a search and clear mission near the village of Duc Tan, in northern South Vietnam when he was mortally wounded. Thus came to an end, in a far away land, the life of one of Florida State's most overachieving athletes.

Center 1963-1966

FOREWORD

Legendary Coach Bobby Bowden

I have been asked to do an introductory preview and commentary about this book, entitled "Sons of the Sixties — A Case for the Defense," co-authored by two former Seminole football players, Johnny Crowe and Dale McCullers. I was intrigued with the concept of this book from the very beginning, because in the book, Johnny and Dale have captured a wonderful bygone era of Seminole football, the decade of the 1960s.

As the title reflects, aspiring young athletes who played football for the Seminoles in the 1960s, came to FSU as the young adult children of the so-called Greatest Generation, so nicknamed by Tom Brokaw, a former NBC anchorman. The parents of these young men surely earned this distinction because of faithfully enduring and prevailing over the Great Depression in America and World War II.

In my experience as a now retired Florida State University head coach, Johnny and Dale have also captured a unique theme for their book, concentrating on the critical role **defense** plays in developing championship caliber football teams across the American college landscape. From my perspective as a former head coach of a past National Championship team, the Florida State Seminoles, I can say unequivocally that it was my own unwavering commitment and coaching philosophy to place some of my toughest and fastest players on the defensive side of the line of scrimmage.

It would have been virtually impossible to establish a winning tradition at FSU, without a solid defensive scheme and talented defensive players.

I used to tell my defensive players, "if the opponent can't score, and our offense can, they can't win." I encourage all sports fans, plus anyone else who enjoys a good book, to read "Sons of the Sixties — A Case for the Defense." This book will help the average fan to really understand the mental and physical toughness required to become a college or pro level defensive football player. It is obvious Johnny and Dale have labored many long hours to highlight the remarkable achievements of a stellar group of Seminole athletes which are mentioned throughout this book. They also provide interesting commentary by many FSU defensive coaches of the past, including emphasizing core values and lessons learned and team takeaways gleaned from the game of football, which could very well help you in these difficult and challenging times.

I found this book to be interesting, thought provoking, and historically accurate. I encourage you to read and enjoy this book. I sure did.

Bobby Bowden

INTRODUCTION
A Decade to Remember

In trying to describe the 1960s era of football at FSU, many things come to mind. In some ways, this decade simply faded away as a western sunset does on a balmy summer afternoon.

As one decade passes, another comes along. The past season is quickly replaced by another exciting season on our modern college football landscape. However, to the many fans, coaches, and players of this era, to us at least, the 1960s was truly a decade to remember. Believe it or not, this was a very fun and exciting time at FSU. To those who remember, it's even more interesting and exciting in some respects than college football is today. Many will disagree with this sentiment, but to the fans and players of this decade, it was the best of times. It was also in the similitude of an even burgeoning work in progress on several fronts. To the players themselves, it was an exciting day and age to just line up and play college football.

On game day, there were great players on both sides of the field of play at Doak Campbell Stadium. In the 1960s, the fan base and stadium were smaller, but not the playing field or the players' work ethic and competitive spirit. At this time in its storied history, FSU played against teams like Texas A&M, University of Florida (UF), University of Miami (UM), Louisiana State University (LSU), University of Alabama (UA), Penn State, University of Georgia (UGA), and Virginia Tech, to name a few. In brief, there was very heavy competition among high school and college football teams of that day, as well as other athletic programs at every level on the American sports scene.

The decade of the 1960s had great fans, great players, and, for the most part, great seasons. There were many exciting wins and a few devastating losses. Year by year, and season by season, as the decade rolled on, there always seemed to be an unwavering spirit of optimism among the FSU players and fan base. Through it all, there were always exciting game day experiences to cheer for and special players to watch. It seemed to most of us as if all of the FSU players and fans alike came to games to display a combined high energy and enthusiasm for the game. Each year, new and exciting players and some future stars emerged. Many achieved a measure of greatness before their final senior season at FSU. Several FSU All-Americans and many Athletic Hall of Fame players performed in an exceptional way and not-so-quietly emerged and then moved on. Many players went on to play professional football following their final season at FSU.

During the 1960s, America was also emerging as a world power. It was the post-World War II era, the beginning of a new age and a period of significant growth and achievement in our country, albeit mingled with periods of great sadness and anxiety. During this often volatile and changing decade, John F. Kennedy was assassinated, the Vietnam War began, and England's renowned band, the Beatles, dominated the radio and television airways. College football in the 1960s provided a form of relief from the difficult period and changing attitude about the Vietnam War.

Like every college football team today, the team rosters of the 1960s, were made up of players of many diverse talents and personalities. Unfortunately, in the game of life, many talented players fell to the wayside. The follies of youth, coupled with poor grades, poor judgment, or poor decisions claimed many victims throughout college football nationwide. There were also many talented players who fell prey to career-ending injuries, untimely accidents, illness, and even death during this decade. The one constant seemed to be the beacon of hope in the heartbeats of every fan, coach, and player. Just as it does today, teamwork, unity of purpose, and the unconquerable spirit of Osceola permeated the FSU campus during the 1960s.

In the following pages of this book, the reader will be introduced to the standout players of each season beginning with the late 1950s and culminating in 1970. We hope you will enjoy reading this book as much as the authors, editors, and clerical help enjoyed producing it.

GO NOLES!

> John B. Crowe, Defensive Back and
> Dale G. McCullers, Linebacker, 1965-1968

PREFACE

Starting in the late 1950s and continuing through the entire decade of the 1960s, Seminole fans will be introduced to a wonderful group of athletes from a bygone era of Florida State football.

Our featured FSU Athletic Hall of Fame players' collegiate careers are chronicled and illustrated, along with summaries of their individual lifetime achievements. We have also included a "Coaches Corner" and "Team Takeaway" section to provide additional insights from both coaches and players about this exciting period of Seminole football.

This is not just a nostalgic trip down memory lane for fans of Seminole football. Nor is it for self-aggrandizement so that our featured players or coaches may bask for a moment in the glory days of the past. It is our hope that you will discover many new thought-provoking insights about this historic period in Seminole football. Perhaps you may even internalize a few lessons learned from both the game of football and from the game of life. We feel there are many core values and positive character traits that can be gleaned from reading about these exceptional young men we have collectively nicknamed the Sons of The Sixties.

We also pay tribute to the parents of our featured FSU Athletic Hall of Fame players, known in American culture today by the much-heralded moniker, the Greatest Generation. They have been so honored for both enduring, and prevailing over, the immense challenges they faced during the Great Depression and World War II.

It is also our hope you will enjoy the stories and commentary delivered by both FSU coaches and players of this special and exciting era in Seminole football. Although it seems each season of Seminole football produces many outstanding offensive and defensive players, our emphasis in this book will be defensive football.

There is no doubt that FSU has produced many great offensive stars in its much-celebrated and storied history. However, it seems many great FSU defensive players are somewhat overlooked in terms of highlighting their major contributions to FSU football in both the past and the present. The ongoing trend is for the defense to play a more dominant role in developing championship-caliber football teams. In this book, we make our Case for the Defense and leave it up to you to deliberate and decide. After reading the book, let us know if we have convinced you, or not, that defense really matters in the ongoing search for yet another National Championship at FSU.

John B. Crowe and Dale G. McCullers

PART 1

Background and Theme

CHAPTER 1

THE PARENTS OF THE SONS
OF THE SIXTIES

Dale McCullers

In recent years, there has been much ado about the book written by former NBC Anchorman, Tom Brokaw entitled "The Greatest Generation." In his book, Mr. Brokaw chronicles the poignant life experiences of many military veterans during the Great Depression, World War II, and early post-war America.

In his book, the reader gets many insightful peeks into the lives of these brave men and women who were born in the 1920s. Many of these noble Americans have passed away and are no longer part of modern American life. Through mini-biographies and related commentary, his book tells stories about those who endured the Great Depression, fought in World War II, and went on to lay the foundation stones for thrift and industry in modern America.

During the post-war era, the children born to these illustrious parents were collectively known as baby boomers. These children grew up under the character-building tutelage and leadership of the Greatest Generation from the late 1940s to the early 1950s. Fortunately for them and the FSU fan base, many of these young men made their way to the FSU campus as football players. Hereafter, the authors will refer to these young men as the Sons of the Sixties to differentiate between parent and child.

In subsequent chapters in this book, the reader will be introduced to an extraordinary group of young men who played college football at Florida State University. Right now, we wish to pay special tribute to the Greatest Generation, or to the fine parents of these young men. Thanks to Mr. Brokaw, we already know these parents as the Greatest Generation. It goes without saying that all of these Sons of the Sixties recognize and honor their parents' legacy. We all share the view that they were a tremendous group of men and women who deserve our honor and respect. Their individual and collective body of work far exceeds the stature or fame of any American athlete or gridiron competitor. We honorably acknowledge their sacrifices and challenges of daily life, sometimes living in the relative poverty and extremism in which the Greatest Generation endured and prevailed. Truly, the life and times of these noble men and women were devoted to God, family, and country, and the greater cause of mankind.

The Greatest Generation were not the world's most perfect parents. They would be the first to admit it. It is assumed the heavens will not be filled with humans who never made mistakes; this includes the Greatest Generation. Using the intellectual and emotional fuel of their own upbringing, however, they schooled their children to accept reality, to deal with and overcome adversity, and to build character and integrity into their daily lives.

Unfortunately, many of these noble warriors of the past have gone and are still dying at an alarming rate. All of us sometimes forget in the press of daily life the natural deterioration process going on in our minds and bodies. We all forget details as we age. As we grow older we experience "senior moments" and forget details about things like athletic competition, rival teams, wins and losses, coaches and players' names, and team records. Many game day memories, like exciting wins or embarrassing losses, seem to fade with time and drift away like a cloud on the horizon. However, what isn't forgotten or lost is our memories of our parents. Our parents were highly ethical, hard-working, selfless people with well-defined core values, and they passed that on.

The Sons of the Sixties also persevered and prevailed through some pretty tough life experiences and some equally intense football competition. We were there when the first American astronauts landed on the moon. We were there when John F. Kennedy was assassinated. We were there when we beat our biggest rival, the Florida Gators, in 1964 in Tallahassee. We were there when we beat the Gators again, this time in the infamous Swamp in Gainesville, Florida in 1967. We were also there when we tied the number one team in the nation, Alabama, in Tuscaloosa in 1967 with a final score of 37-37.

But I'm getting ahead of myself — just read the book.

CHAPTER 2

A CASE FOR THE DEFENSE

John B. Crowe

Football at Florida State University is about defense. After World War II, solders returning from defending our freedoms took advantage of the G.I. Bill to attend college. Those coming to Florida put stress on the university system, causing the quick opening of the Tallahassee Branch of the University of Florida (TBUF) on the campus of Florida State College for Women (FSCW). Over 900 men were enrolled at TBUF. By 1947, the Florida Legislature turned FSCW into a co-educational college and renamed Florida State College for Women - Florida State University. The university president at that time, Doak Campbell, saw the opportunity and need for a football team to keep the men occupied, and so football began at FSU. Fast forward 70 years ...

In early November 2017, Florida State University hosted a 50th year milestone reunion for the 1967 Seminole football team. The weekend was full of activities for returning teammates, including a reception in the Varsity Club at Doak Campbell Stadium and Bobby Bowden Field, with a gathering at the indoor football facility, participation in the traditional Sod Cemetery Talk, team introductions, an on-field ceremony during half-time of the FSU — Syracuse game, and a team reception following the game.

During the weekend, Dale McCullers shared his concern that it seems as if defensive players of the 1960s have been forgotten, or at least not remembered as vividly as the offensive players from that period. Dale commented that I should write a book about my experiences in life and how playing defensive back at FSU influenced my careers in the military and forest products industry. While I was flattered that Dale thought my life might be of interest to someone, I passed it off and believed I didn't have the time.

Dale wrote me a thank you note for the help I had provided FSU setting up the weekend activities and hosting the post-game reception. He later telephoned me and asked if I would consider co-authoring a book about defensive players from the 1960s, suggesting that we should take the time to recognize many of our former teammates that are being forgotten. Dale made the case for recognizing the Sons of the Sixties and their parents, the so-called Greatest Generation, for the sacrifices they made in World War II, so their children — the first of the baby boomers — could have a better life through education and increased opportunities provided by experiences at a university.

I reconnected in person with Dale on December 6, 2017, several weeks after the team reunion when he traveled to Thomasville, Georgia to visit a dying teammate of ours, Chuck Eason. Chuck made it to the reunion through sheer willpower and determination and subsequently passed away on December 14, 2017. During lunch with Dale that day, he and I discussed the idea of this project. It was obvious that Dale had the unbridled passion for the effort, and his enthusiasm was contagious! I discussed it with my wife, Betty, who was extremely encouraging. While I originally believed I didn't have time to work on this, I came to the realization that I didn't have time NOT to work on it.

I believe three things convinced me that this was worthwhile. First, Dale's and Betty's passion that this would be a great thing! Second, our 1967 team has already lost 17 players (as of this writing), and three of them died in 2017. I believe that some of their lives were likely shortened by injuries suffered playing football. The third and final reason was that, even if the book was never published, working with Dale to document the history of many defensive players from the 1960s would be a great life experience — probably the greatest value of all.

It is not our intention to take away from any offensive player in the 1960s or to not recognize all of the men who played during those years. The purpose of "A Case for the Defense" is to recognize the Sons of the Sixties who came to FSU in the 1960s and took advantage of the sacrifices that their parents made to give them such an opportunity. I hope you will enjoy the book and not judge us as biased because we played defense but rather appreciate the efforts to document the lives of many of our defensive team-mates. It is our hope that all of our teammates will appreciate the outcome and feel part of the emotion and passion that we felt writing it.

Lee Corso - Defensive Back 1953 - 1956

CHAPTER 3

AN EMERGING MINISTER OF DEFENSE

Dale McCullers

A TWO-WAY STAR IS BORN

Growing up in northern Florida about an hour from Tallahassee, I knew at a very young age that FSU football was a big deal. The FSU campus was near downtown Tallahassee and close to the Florida State Capitol. In the early 1950s, this area of the state was known as the Big Bend Region of Florida. My family's allegiance was to the Florida Gators, since the University of Florida campus was only 60 miles away in nearby Gainesville, Florida. Little did I know that I would one day break family tradition and play football for the Florida State Seminoles.

In 1956, I turned 9 years old, and in every decade thereafter up to this present day, I have been an ardent FSU fan. As a young boy, I was particularly enthused about — no, idolized — an FSU player by the name of Lee Corso. Although there were other great players on the team, Lee Corso, affectionately known as "The Sunshine Scooter," became a household name around my hometown of Live Oak, Florida.

It is fitting and very gratifying to me personally that Lee Corso was the first FSU player to be recognized as a true defensive star at FSU. Although there were many great defensive players who also distinguished themselves in the decades to follow, Lee was clearly one of the best. As a two-way starter on both defense and offense, he is probably one of the most versatile athletes to ever play for the Seminoles. One thing is clear: it would be hard to imagine anyone exceeding Lee's lifetime career achievements or match his extraordinary contributions to the game of college football. We will now continue our commentary below on the irrepressible Lee Corso and his amazing life.

LEE CORSO'S EARLY LIFE & COLLEGIATE CAREER

Lee was born on August 7th, 1935, the son of Italian immigrants. Lee and his parents settled in the Miami, Florida area in the early 1950s. Beginning around 1952, Lee first played quarterback for Miami Jackson Senior High School. He was also a baseball prospect who, in his senior year, was offered a $5,000 signing bonus to play shortstop for the Brooklyn Dodgers. At the time, Lee was one of the most highly recruited athletes in FSU history. Lee was known for his exceptional versatility and quickness in high school.

He probably could have gone to any team in the nation, but fortunately for FSU fans, Lee chose to play college football and baseball for the Seminoles instead of playing for the Dodgers. While at FSU, Lee earned the nickname "Sunshine Scooter" for his speed and style of play, which was always exciting to watch. Early in his FSU career, Lee was a roommate of running back, and later actor, Burt Reynolds.

As a defensive star, Lee set the school record for interceptions at 14, an exceptional accomplishment in any era. This record stood for two decades. He led FSU players in interceptions in 1954, in rushing in 1955, and passing in 1956. This type of versatility is mostly unheard of on the modern sports scene. What makes his defensive role as an FSU cornerback so unique is that he was also a star running back and quarterback for the Seminoles. His highlight film was recorded on both sides of the field due to his exceptional style of play. Lee was tough, quick, agile, and savvy, all at the same time. His tenacity as a cornerback and superb acumen for diagnosing plays was unequaled in his era.

Lee was inducted into the FSU Athletic Hall of Fame in 1978 and the following is the citation for his selection:

> Lee Corso came to Florida State in 1953 as one of the most highly recruited players in Florida history. He starred on both offense and defense on the football field leading the Seminoles in interceptions in 1954, rushing in 1955, and passing in 1956. He was the FSU career interception leader with 14 until Deion Sanders tied him in the late 1980s. He was honorable mention All-American (Associated Press) as a senior in 1956 and selected to play in the Blue-Gray All-Star game. Corso also played in the outfield on the Seminole baseball team. After graduation, he became an assistant football coach at Florida State, Maryland, and Navy before becoming head coach at Louisville and Indiana. Corso then transitioned to television broadcasting, becoming a household name as ESPN's top football analyst.

Even more amazing than his football skill was what Lee accomplished after graduating from FSU. Most Americans now know Lee as a legendary figure in American sports broadcasting history. How did Lee accomplish his amazing rise to become a legendary figure in sports broadcasting? After first graduating with a bachelor's degree in physical education and a master's degree in administration and supervision — both from FSU — Lee spent the following three decades serving as an assistant coach at FSU, Maryland, and Navy before accepting head coaching jobs at Louisville, Indiana, and the USFL Orlando Renegades.

In 1987, following his stellar 28-year coaching career at the college and professional level, Lee Corso joined ESPN's College GameDay as a sports analyst. This seven-time Emmy Award-winning show features Lee as one of the most knowledgeable and entertaining sports broadcasters in modern sports history. In addition to multiple Emmy Awards for College GameDay, Sporting News magazine awarded Lee and fellow GameDay co-hosts, Chris Fowler and Kirk Herbstreit, 2003's "Most Powerful Media Personalities in Sports." As College GameDay's national appeal has skyrocketed, Lee's analysis and predictions about the outcome of games involving major football rivalries is both highly interesting and entertaining. His GameDay analysis and opinions have become much anticipated news for college sports fans throughout America. Lee remains a fan favorite. Who can forget Lee's wonderful catchphrase — "Not so fast my friend" — as he challenges his co-hosts regarding the predictions and outcomes of upcoming games? Lee's amusing antics, like donning university mascot headgear and either riling or pleasing TV fans, is always lively and enjoyable.

Lee Corso has genuinely earned the many prestigious honors he has received, such as the Ronald Reagan Media Award for outstanding sports broadcasting, and he has earned the respect of all who know him. He is also a member of the Florida State, Indiana, Kentucky, and Louisville University's Halls of Fame and was inducted into the FSU Alumni Association's "Circle of Gold," the highest alumni honor. FSU fans are forever grateful Lee chose to play college football at Florida State. Lee Corso is simply an All-Time Seminole great.

Tony Romeo - Defensive End 1957 -1960

CHAPTER 4
PROFESSIONAL ROLE MODEL

John B. Crowe

In the early 1960s, FSU had only two notable players in the professional football ranks: Tony Romeo and Bud Whitehead. The two were teammates and had been drafted in 1961. At the end of the decade, that number would climb to nine. Going into the 2018 season, the number of FSU former players on NFL rosters is north of 50! Tony and Bud led the way and were important role models, Tony with the Boston Patriots and Bud with the San Diego Chargers. They would represent FSU well in pro football and in the way they lived their lives.

The remarkable college and professional football career of FSU defensive end Tony Romeo is not as well-known, and maybe somewhat overlooked, by the modern day FSU fan base, due to the bygone era in which he played. However, the older generation of fans, former teammates, and coaches truly recognize and appreciate Tony as one of the most brilliant two-way starters to ever don a garnet and gold uniform. He made a strong case for the defense!

Highly recruited out of Hillsborough High School in Tampa, Florida in 1956-57, Tony played both offensive and defensive end for the Seminoles. Tony was one of the first bona fide blue-chip players to come to FSU. Lee Corso was an assistant coach at FSU and recruited Tony. In the press guide following Tony's freshman year, he was described with the following credits:

> An offensive and defensive standout in the spring game ... he scored two touchdowns and could be the best sophomore in Seminole history ... a gifted pass receiver who likes defense even better ... he has the potential to be one of the best ends in America ... needs experience ... no question about ability.

By the standards of the 1950s and 1960s, Tony was considered a big kid, standing 6'3" and tipping the scales at 224 pounds. In 1958, he would be the largest player on the roster. The size of players today has certainly changed, but back then, he was what they called a biggin! He would trim down to 200 pounds in his senior year. In the 30 games that Tony appeared for the Seminoles, he started at the offensive and defensive end 24 times. Tony would finish his college career as the team captain on the first team and season of the Bill Peterson era. During the 1958, 1959, and 1960 seasons, Tony excelled for the Seminoles, earning AP and UPI All-American (Honorable Mention) honors, as well as being named the Florida Defensive Lineman of the Week three times, an unprecedented and impressive achievement for any era of football.

Drafted by the Washington Redskins in the 19th round in 1961, Tony played professional football for seven years in the AFL, initially with the Dallas Texans and then with the Boston Patriots. He dramatically excelled, once again, as an offensive tight end for the Patriots. In 1966, over 50 years ago, Tony was named Florida Pro Athlete of the Year for making a record 10 catches for 149 yards in a single game for the Boston Patriots, a record he still holds. Tony was inducted into the Florida State Athletic Hall of Fame in 1988, and this was the citation to accompany his selection:

> Former defensive end Tony Romeo is best known for a sophomore season in 1958 that produced honorable mention All-American honors from the Associated Press and United Press International. Romeo keyed a strong FSU defensive effort that led to an appearance in the Bluegrass Bowl. He was named Florida Defensive Line-

man of the Week three times. Although he was often injured in his junior and senior seasons, Romeo played both ways for the Garnet and Gold, making the Florida All-State team as a senior. After being drafted by the Washington Redskins and traded to the Boston Patriots, Romeo played seven years for the Pats. He still holds the tight end record for catches in a game (10 for 149 yards) and was Florida's Pro Athlete of the Year in 1966.

Romeo was also known for beginning the first chapel services in professional football. Following his pro career, he spent time in the ministry before putting his FSU business degree to work.

His performance helped the Patriots reach the AFL Title Game in 1963. He was a favorite target of legendary quarterback Babe Parilli because of his "sure hands" and ability to run disciplined pass routes. In the 1962 season, he had a career high 34 catches for 608 yards. It is worth noting that the Patriots' opponent in the 1963 Title Game was the San Diego Chargers, and Tony competed against former Seminole teammate Bud Whitehead. That was special for both of them and for all Seminoles! Tony would go on to play 89 regular season games, compiling 117 receptions for 1,813 yards and 10 touchdowns. Notable is his significant career average of 15.5 yards per reception!

Tony passed away in May 1996 at the young age of 58. He fought cancer for many years and continued his ministry until the end. He is the only defensive FSU Athletic Hall of Fame player in our book we were not able to interview. We have relied on what has been written about his athletic performance and life. Briefly I will provide some highlights:

Tony was raised in the St. Petersburg - Tampa area by his parents Anthony and Martha Romeo. He was named Anthony Lamar Romeo after his father and being an only child, he had the full attention of his parents. His father served as a Corporal in the U.S. Army and a WWII Veteran, and I imagine that Tony grew up with many of the same family values and faith as other Sons of the Sixties. However, Tony experienced tough times as a youth and ran with the Orient Gang, having territorial disputes with other gangs.

Because of his size, he was feared. Like the others in our book, Tony excelled in sports and used his athletic ability to move forward and further his education. It was while attending FSU on a football scholarship that Tony was influenced by some good men of Tallahassee like LeRoy Collins, Dean Mode Stone, and Baptist Minister Rev. Harold Sandes, turning his life to become a Christian. He along with a few other teammates established the Fellowship of Christian Athletes. Following his professional football career, he would attain a master's degree from the Southern Baptist Theological Seminary. Always a role model of demonstrated strong faith, Tony had the distinction of initiating the first chapel services in professional football and was a leader for the evangelical movement among professional football players. During the off-season and following his retirement, Tony would travel widely speaking in churches. While his life was short, he made an impact using his business degree from Florida State University, his faith, and ministry to witness to others. In 2001, Tony was inducted into Hillsborough High School's first Hall of Fame Class. Tony married Sabra (Briggs) Romeo whom he met at a Christian Retreat, and they had two daughters and two grandsons. The family lived in the Charlotte, North Carolina community, and he is buried in Burnsville, North Carolina.

Number 80, Anthony Lamar Romeo is gone but not forgotten, and he will always be a great role model! He was tireless and fearless on the football field and in his ministry. Although I never met Tony Romeo, I feel like I know him and admire his courage and accomplishments. He practiced what he preached.

Bud Whitehead - Defensive Back 1957-1960

CHAPTER 5

MR. VERSATILITY

John B. Crowe

Rubin Angus (Bud) Whitehead was Florida State's early version of Deion Sanders. He was likely one of the most versatile players to ever wear garnet and gold. He played running back and defensive back and led the team in receptions and interceptions. When it came to special teams, he returned both punts and kick-offs and did the punting. If he had a few spare moments, he could have sold popcorn and played in the FSU Marching Chiefs. Oh yeah, Bud also lettered in basketball at FSU, but let's start at the beginning.

Bud was born on January 1, 1939, the second of six children to Clara and Alter Whitehead. Bud was named Rubin for his grandfather and Angus for the doctor who delivered him. He got the name "Bud" because he grew up playing sports with his older brother, Jim, and the boys in the neighborhood called him "little buddy," which was later shortened to Bud. He claims that because he grew up playing with older boys, when it came time to play with boys his own age, he had a significant advantage that allowed him to excel.

I had a memorable experience sitting in Bud and Diana Whitehead's living room in Fresno, California and getting the chance to listen to a very humble role model for me, and likely many others, talk about his life. He grew up in a Christian family of eight during a difficult time in our history.

While his family had no money, they always had food and plenty of love to go around.

COACH'S COMMENT   "A very versatile and talented athlete. Good coach that you respected because he had played the game and was a successful pro!" — Coach Wyant

Bud's parents met and were raised in Cottonwood, Alabama. They moved to Marianna, Florida because Bud's grandfather had found work there and asked them to give the city a try. Bud remembers life in Marianna as a safe and peaceful time. He said,

> You didn't have to lock the doors because everyone knew you and there wasn't any crime. If you left your ball glove or basketball outside it would be there in the morning. We didn't have television, so you played sports, picked cotton, and went to bed. We traveled to football or basketball games every Friday or Saturday night somewhere in a 30-mile radius of Marianna and the Methodist Church every Sunday. That was what we did and always as a family.

I found his comments about Marianna being a safe haven to be interesting. I told Bud that where I was raised, any time a boy got in trouble, the school principal would threaten to send him to Marianna. For years, Marianna was the location of the State Reform School for Boys. We had a good laugh together about our different impressions of the same place.

Bud's role models were his parents and his older brother, Jim. They taught him to work hard and encouraged him in sports. His mother may have been the best athlete in the family, and she excelled at basketball. Bud developed skills in football, basketball, and baseball, and he credits his versatility to playing on teams few in numbers. Bud learned to do it all: punt, pass, catch, run, and return kicks. This would be the hallmark of his athletic career and how he came to be called Mr. Versatility.

His parents wanted their children to have the opportunities that higher education could provide. Bud's father, like many of the men of the 1930s and

1940s, didn't complete high school because he had to work and support his family. His mother completed high school before dedicating herself to raising the family, but she didn't go to college. When recruiting letters from several colleges started to arrive, Bud and his parents saw it as his chance for greater opportunities. He would need the scholarship to afford college. With their encouragement, Bud chose FSU, luckily for us!

Bud left Marianna in 1957 to begin his freshman year at Florida State University. He played both football and basketball while at FSU, and, looking back, could have been a three-sport letterman, a very rare accomplishment. Another teammate on Bud's high school team would also follow him to FSU, quarterback Bobby Conrad. Bud speaks with admiration for Bobby, praising his football skills and what could have been. Bobby was tragically killed in an automobile accident in 1959. Bud's brother, Willie, would team with Bud and the Seminoles in 1959 as a running back and defensive back. Bud would be the first college graduate in his family, and his brothers and sister would follow. Bud's younger brothers, Gary and Ronnie, would follow Bud and Willie to FSU.

In the years that Bud played at FSU, the substitution rule required most players to play both offense and defense. Bud starred on both sides of the ball and on special teams. Not often does a player lead the team in receptions and interceptions, as well as punting and returning both kick-offs and punts. When you examine the results, he did it all very well!

1959 was a break-out year for Bud. His performance against Virginia Tech that year was key to a hard fought 7-6 victory. He intercepted three passes that day, a feat only performed a few times in FSU's 70 years of football. He also led the nation that year with six interceptions, a remarkable number given that most teams of that era didn't throw more than 10 passes in a game. One memorable interception that year was Bud's interception of the celebrated quarterback Norm Snead's pass and his dazzling zig-zag return of 81 yards for a touchdown against Wake Forest. Bud set new single game and season records with 9 catches against Tampa and 31 receptions for the season. Bud's stats for 1959 truly proved his versatility: 46 rushes for 148 yards and one touchdown, 31 receptions for 320 yards and two touchdowns, three kick-off returns for 64 yards, nine punt returns for 64 yards, 29 punts with average of 36.9 yards, and six pass interceptions with one touchdown. Bud must have only taken off his helmet for the National Anthem, because the rest of the time he was on the field! He was like an Energizer battery — he just kept going and going!

In 1960, Coach Bill Peterson became the head coach, inheriting a team without much depth. In his first year, Coach Pete depended on Bud for leadership and big plays. It didn't take long for Seminole fans to get excited about the new brand of football that Coach Peterson was bringing to Tallahassee. On the opening kick-off that year, Bud received the kick and handed it to Eddy Feely, who lateraled to Carl Meyer. This was the first of many trick plays the Seminoles used in the 11 years that Coach Pete was Florida State's head coach. The season started well in 1960 and included a disappointing but hard fought 3-0 loss to the Gators. The wins over Richmond, Wake Forest, William and Mary, and a tie with TCU had the team positioned for a winning season. The Seminoles dropped their last four games to Kentucky, Miami, Houston, and Auburn. Bill Peterson's first year was not a winning season. However, Bud's performance was remarkable. Bud had performed a rare feat, leading the team in rushing, receiving, and scoring with 81 rushes for 293 yards and two touchdowns, 23 receptions for 204 yards and one touchdown. He punted 53 times during the season and returned kick-offs and punts. He was picked by his coaches as the most valuable player, won the Tallahassee Quarterback Club award for leadership, and was chosen to play in the North-South College All-Star game.

In 1961, the San Diego Chargers — an AFL team —drafted Bud as a defensive back, and he played eight seasons with the Chargers. He played in 94 games and had 15 interceptions and one touchdown. He continued to return punts and even did some punting. Bud played in four AFL Championship Games, including the 1963 AFL Championship Game, ultimately beating the Boston Patriots 51-10. He is remembered for his sure tackling and competitive attitude. Bud recalls the pro football experience with pride and satisfaction. He valued his teammates and his relationship with two outstanding mentors and coaches: head coach Sid Gillman and position coach Chuck Noll. Bud speaks of both with admiration and appreciation for the influence they had on his life. They both took interest in their players and built caring relationships.

In 1981, Bud Whitehead was elected to the FSU Athletic Hall of Fame. The citation that accompanied the award read:

> Versatility is the word that best summarizes the FSU athletic career of Bud Whitehead. He lettered in both football and basketball. On the gridiron, Bud Whitehead was a brilliant two-way player. In 1959, he led the Seminoles in both pass receptions and pass interceptions. His six interceptions led the nation and his 31 receptions placed him 8th nationally. Both these marks were FSU records, as were his nine receptions and three interceptions in a single game. In 1960, Whitehead was chosen FSU's most valuable football player. After his senior year in 1960, Whitehead played in the North-South All-Star game. Following graduation, the Marianna native starred with the San Diego Chargers, making a reputation as one of the hardest hitting defensive backs in the NFL. In 1969 and 1970, Whitehead returned to his alma mater as an assistant offensive coach. College and pro athlete and coach, Bud Whitehead represents the best in Seminole athletics.

Sitting and listening to Bud talk, I came away with great respect for him, with his genuine humility and his love of family. I drove from Hollywood, California to see Bud face-to-face. As a small town guy with small town driving skills, I braved the California experience and intimidation of Highway 405, Interstate 5, and Highway 99 to get to Fresno and back. Eight hours of terror and traffic jams were tense, but the two hours with Bud and his wife Diana made the adventure worth the gray hairs.

Here is what I learned that day in Fresno:

Bud had a very successful career in the Food Sales and Logistics Industry and this brought him to one of the greatest areas with fertile lands to grow food crops: Fresno, California and the San Joaquin Valley. He is now retired and has lived in the same home for 42 years. Their property and neighborhood is beautifully landscaped. When asked what he considered his greatest achievement in life, he didn't hesitate and replied, "My family!" He credits football for bringing him and Diana together. Drafted by the Chargers, he would start his pro career in San Diego. They met in San Diego and have been married for 55 years. They have three children, eight grandchildren, and two great-grandchildren. When asked what he would like to be remembered for, he replied, "That I always gave my best on and off the field. I didn't hold anything back."

He credits his football experiences for his life successes:

> Football provided learnings about self-discipline and how to be a team player that made a difference in my career. I developed many lifelong and lasting friendships. Those friends have made me a better person. While we didn't make the kind of money the players make today, pro football provided the foundation that allowed Diana and I to grow together and live a comfortable and satisfying life.

During the off-season for Bud in 1967, he helped coach defensive backs at FSU in spring training. That was the first time I met him as a player and remember that he seemed "bigger than life" to me with his pro football player experience — I was in awe! I am still in awe 51 years later!

Today, Bud enjoys golf, but more often than not, he can be found at the local hospital or rescue mission coaching and counseling others who are dealing with many of life's issues. Bud and Diana support the Gideon Bible Ministry. They have a strong faith, and their faith has helped them through the good and also the difficult times.

Bud is truly a credit to Florida State University and to his family. Bud and Diana return to Marianna each year at Labor Day for a family and friends reunion. He still has a passion for his hometown! Bud represents what Dale and I wanted to capture with our book: he comes from parents of the

Greatest Generation and has carried their values on to create a successful life and family of his own. Leaving Marianna for FSU, he wasn't sure he could compete at the next level or on a bigger stage. His discipline, determination, preparedness, and strong work ethic made the difference. He is a great example of our Case for the Defense.

Gene McDowell - Linebacker 1959 - 1961

CHAPTER 6

WAYCROSS WARRIOR

John B. Crowe

Ephraim Eugene McDowell was born on July 4, 1940 to a modest, hardworking Christian family. He grew up in Waycross, Georgia in a small town environment where life and times were difficult, but nobody complained or talked about it. Gene says, "That was just the way it was. Everyone accepted it and got on with life."

Gene McDowell came from a family that understood hardships and challenges. His great-great grandfather was John K. McLane, an early settler in what today is Gadsden County, Florida. I read a story about Mr. McLane and his experiences during the Creek War in 1840 and his service in the American Civil War. Mr. McLane was present at Appomattox Courthouse in April 1865. The title of the article said it all, "Tough Living, Hard Dying." Gene's family heritage is that of true grit! Coach McDowell is the epitome of discipline and toughness.

His father enlisted in the Army during World War II. He served in the Pacific, experiencing some of the most aggressive fighting in the battle of Okinawa. Wounded in the chest, the bullet was never removed because of where it was lodged, so his dad healed and carried the bullet the rest of his life. Gene's role models growing up were his dad and his football coach. Gene developed a strong work ethic early and remembers "throwing and turning" tobacco to earn money for school supplies and clothes. He also worked in a lumber mill and was assigned to the area known as the "hole" or "dugout." In those days, the sawmill sawyer determined what to cut out of a log, and he could work the guy in the "hole" to complete exhaustion by sending lumber and slabs faster than they could be sorted into the correct product line — you would have to be there to appreciate it. It was a great job to produce persistence, endurance, and a passion for getting an education. Gene developed his toughness early in life, and it has served him well. Gene would follow in the footsteps of both of his role models, serving as military police in the Army in Okinawa and working as a coach. He speaks with pride about his family, service to country and his coaching experiences.

Gene was a great high school athlete and football star. He chose Florida State University because of his admiration for his high school coach, W.A. (Dub) Kendrick. Coach Kendrick was a member of FSU's first football team. Gene was a team leader, and as a college sophomore, he teamed with Bud Whitehead on Coach Bill Peterson's first year as FSU's head football coach. While Coach Pete's first year wasn't a winning season, Seminole fans sensed the dawning of a new style of football. When recruiting was over following the 1960 season, some of the names that were drawn to FSU were Winfred Bailey, Jack Edwards, Bill "Red" Dawson, Jack Shinholser, Avery Sumner, Steve Tensi, and a young man from Erie, Pennsylvania named Fred Biletnikoff. These players joined with upperclassmen to make history in 1964. Gene would not be on that team, but he set a standard for all with his discipline and toughness!

He starred on the 1961 and 1962 Seminoles as an offensive guard and linebacker. He led the team in tackles and was selected team captain his senior year. Gene was recognized as one of the finest linebackers in FSU history. His junior year, he was recognized as Florida Lineman of the Week for his 17 tackles against Southern Mississippi. He led his teammates in a 3-3 tie with Florida, a win over Georgia in 1961, and three ties in 1962 with Kentucky, Auburn, and Georgia Tech.

COACH'S COMMENT

"Mentally tough and no nonsense guy!" — Coach Wyant

Gene would go on to become FSU's first recognized All-American in 1962, when he led his team to the first winning season under Coach Bill Peterson. Gene's honors that year included AP's third team All-American squad, Quarterback Club trophy (given annually to a senior for team leadership), and Florida's College Player of the Year. The 1962 team made a Case for the Defense! The defense gave up only 69 points in 10 games against a difficult and tough schedule. They held four teams scoreless! Vince Gibson, one of Gene's coaches and the first FSU graduate to become a major college head coach, described Gene as the most dedicated athlete he had the pleasure to coach at FSU. Following graduation, Gene went on to serve his country in the Army before starting his coaching career in 1965 as an assistant coach of the FSU freshman team. Coach Gibson would later hire Gene as an assistant coach at Kansas State for several years before Gene returned to coach defensive ends and linebackers at Florida State.

I believe one of the greatest honors for anyone is to be called "Coach" because it is out of great respect and appreciation. That is how I feel about Coach McDowell. I met Coach McDowell in August 1965, when I reported to the football locker room to begin my career as a Seminole football player. Coach called me by my name and welcomed me to college football. Later that week, he introduced me, along with my teammates, to what we called the "dog days of August" and two-a-day football practices. I still get goose bumps each August when I smell the fresh-mowed grass and have memories about rolling in it during drills and scrimmages. In August of 1965, the temperature was often above 100 degrees, and it was, and always will be, one of the most challenging experiences of my life. Coach McDowell said, "Coach Peterson told the coaches to make these boys tough and we did." Boys that made it through the practice drills and the legendary off-season drills known as "mat drills" were tough. The lessons I learned about stamina to persist, endure, and overcome difficult situations helped me throughout my life and career. My teammates have expressed some of the same feelings. I will always value the experience but wouldn't want to do it again as one time is enough learning for a lifetime.

When discussing Coach McDowell with Dale, we both were impressed by the way he carried himself: he was very self-disciplined, very precise, and very deliberate in his speech, teachings, and demeanor. He would stand with his hands on his hips without an ounce of fat on his body and drill us into superb conditioning. He would tell players, "I don't care if your daddy is rich and your mother is good looking, you gentlemen will be in better shape than your opponent, and we will win in the fourth quarter," and we did!

Time and time again, his teammates said they learned self-discipline and mental toughness observing Coach McDowell play football. Coach McDowell was a no nonsense kind of guy. He always looked you straight in the eye with a twinkle and a smile that were subtle, piercing, and discerning all at the same time. Coach McDowell had the unique ability to point out a player's weaknesses and shortcomings without offending them and then would coach and motivate them to turn their weaknesses into strengths. He didn't baby his players and, although players knew he was tough on them, they knew he cared.

In 1985, Coach McDowell was elected into the Florida State University Athletic Hall of Fame and was recognized with the following citation:

> Gene McDowell came to Florida State from Waycross, Georgia and stayed to become one of the Seminoles' greatest linebackers. McDowell played guard and linebacker from 1960 through 1962. He was captain of the 1962 Seminoles and that season was named to AP's third team All-America, the first FSU player to be so highly honored. In '62, McDowell was named the team's MVP and Florida's College Player of the Year. He also played in the North-South All-Star game.

McDowell coached at FSU in 1968-69 and then moved to Kansas State for four years before returning to Tallahassee where he coached the Tribe linebackers from 1974 to 1984. In 1985, he was named head coach at Central Florida. As player and coach, Gene McDowell has represented the garnet and gold well.

COACH'S COMMENT "I watched him in high school and knew he was physical for a small guy! Tough! A real competitor! Great example of mental and physical toughness." —Coach Bowden

In both of these positions, Gene is a link to FSU's past. Additionally, Coach helped make the football program at the University of Central Florida a nationally recognized program. An Orlando Sentinel article on Coach written by Shannon Green in September 2015 titled "UCF Football Embraces Former Head Coach Gene McDowell," describes a habit Coach had of cornering one or two players during practice and, while chewing on his cigar, he would focus his stern game face and ask a simple question, "So what do you think?" There was no background to the question, and the player or players were often clueless to what his question was about. Players learned just to improvise and come up with something. Mr. Green credits Coach McDowell as the man who saved UCF football from extinction. Coach McDowell is still the winningest head coach in UCF history with an 86-61 record. His UCF boosters and friends have recognized him as a UCF Legend.

Coach left the University of Central Florida in 1997 to return to North Florida. He had a go at coaching the short-lived Tallahassee Arena football team before officially retiring. He became an avid golfer and enjoyed many years of fellowship with friends on several golf courses around Tallahassee and Quincy. He still enjoys having lunch with ex-coaches and friends and debating and sharing opinions on a variety of subjects including college football.

Coach will be remembered as a hard-nosed, demanding motivator. He was feared, loved, and admired by his players. He was deeply private and spoke with quiet confidence. He was always calm in tough situations. Not known for expressing emotion, he was affectionately named the "Iceman." Coach was a tireless worker with a dry wit and sometimes used sarcasm to make his points. His loyalty to his players and friends was unwavering.

While visiting with Coach recently, he credits all the coaches he worked for and with for making him a better coach, person, and leader of young men.

He has so many great memories of teammates, players, and coaches, and his face had a joyful smile as he named people, places, plays, and outcomes he remembered. When asked what he is most proud of, he paused for a moment, likely reflecting on many great memories and then he got that Coach McDowell twinkle in his eye and confident smile on his face and said, "I never lost a wrestling match in the four years I was at Florida State."

I am almost certain Coach didn't lose a wrestling match anywhere, ever! In a battle or difficult time, I would want Coach on my team and in my foxhole. His teammates, players, fellow coaches, and friends will tell you that they were better because of their experiences and relationships with Ephraim Eugene McDowell, the Waycross Warrior, Coach, and the Iceman!

Dick Hermann - Linebacker 1961 - 1964

CHAPTER 7

A MAGNIFICENT LINEBACKER

Dale McCullers

In the mid 1960s, when I was a young teenager living in Live Oak, Florida, I became a huge fan of FSU's Dick Hermann, one of the nation's best college linebackers. Personally speaking, Dick Hermann was much more to me than a college football star. He was more than a good role model. In 1964, I played linebacker for my hometown team, the Suwannee Bulldogs. Then and now, in my opinion and my mind's eye, Dick Hermann was the kind of college linebacker and role model I dreamed of hopefully becoming one day.

After my senior year in high school, my dream unexpectedly came true — with a catch. I was offered a football scholarship by FSU's head recruiter, Don James. I was young and naive. I learned over 30 years later from my high school coach that FSU actually wanted to sign our star running back, Johnny Hurst, who later played professionally for the New York Jets. FSU agreed to sign me only because I was Johnny's best friend. My coach told me that FSU thought I had some potential to develop as a college player, but Johnny was the guy they really wanted. Thanks, Coach for that depressing news.

But anyway, back to the featured player of this chapter: the irrepressible Dick Hermann. For younger readers who may not know much about FSU's Dick Hermann, let me enlighten you. Dick was the starting linebacker for the Seminoles for three consecutive seasons, from 1962 to 1964. He was a little over 6 feet tall and weighed about 210 pounds. He was muscular, rugged, and strong. He possessed both talent and true grit. Dick was not a track star, but he was extremely quick, aggressive, and intelligent. During his college years, Dick can best be described as a complete athlete. A fierce competitor, a good student, and a consummate teammate, he was every college coach's dream come true in a linebacker.

In 1964, his senior season, Dick was honored as FSU's Crenshaw Award winner, given annually to the FSU player with the "biggest heart." His passion for the game and his unique combination of toughness and quickness getting to and tackling ball carriers was hard to match. Dick's style of play was relentless, and he was very exciting to watch on game day. He always gave his best. He was particularly impressive in critical moments and in big games, making many sure tackles, frequently and consistently, as he roamed sideline to sideline.

COACH'S COMMENT   "Good speed and quickness, and a hitter; ideal linebacker." — Coach Bowden

In 1985, Dick was the first of the stellar defensive line nicknamed the "Seven Magnificents" to be inducted into the FSU Athletic Hall of Fame. The following is the citation for his selection:

> In 1962 and '63, the Florida State defense was among the best in the South and in 1964 among the best in the nation. A three-year starter at linebacker and key of that powerful defense was Dick Hermann from Marianna. Few FSU defenders have matched his combination of toughness and quickness. He played well in the big games, Auburn and Kentucky in '62, Auburn in '63, and in '64 in the wins over Florida and Oklahoma. Hermann was a leader of the '64 defense called the "Seven Magnificents" and is the first member of that unit to be inducted into the Hall of Fame. Dick Hermann won the Crenshaw Award in 1964 as the "Seminole with

the biggest heart." Roaming the field from linebacker, Dick Hermann brought honor to the garnet and gold.

As an interesting side note, when Dick was a sophomore and starting linebacker for FSU in 1962, his unspoken mentor and teammate was none other than senior linebacker Gene McDowell, a great FSU linebacker in his own right.

In addition to his football prowess, Dick was a good student and very active in the team and coach-sponsored Fellowship of Christian Athletes. Dick devoted his free time to community service, public speaking, and many other charitable events in the Tallahassee area. Since departing FSU, Dick has remained active in community affairs and true and faithful to his high standards and moral convictions. Dick Hermann was truly an all-time garnet and gold great.

Following graduation from FSU, Dick played professional football for two seasons with the Oakland Raiders, and three seasons with the Orlando Panthers of the Continental Football League. Dick then pursued a career in the private sector, primarily in the corporate insurance industry. Like many other Sons of the Sixties, Dick is now retired. He is a very active senior citizen in his local community and an ardent Seminole fan. He and his wife, Alice, now live in his hometown of Marianna, Florida. He remains a good friend. He is still a great role model for any young man who has a desire to succeed in the game of life.

Jack Shinholser - Nose Tackle 1961-1965

CHAPTER 8

THE WRECKER

Dale McCullers

O ur next featured star athlete, Jack Shinholser, is another renowned
defensive player who played offensive guard, defensive tackle, middle
guard, and linebacker for the Seminoles from 1962 to 1965. Simply
put, Jack Shinholser is one of the most gifted and celebrated athletes in
Florida State history. Highly recruited by FSU as a high school senior,
Jack was an All-City, All-State, and All-American (Honorable Mention)
linebacker at Chamberlain High School in Tampa, Florida before coming to FSU. Although many college teams were actively recruiting Jack,
fortunately for FSU fans, he chose to play for Florida State. During the
1961 season, FSU's head coach, Bill Peterson, was personally involved in
the recruiting process and persuaded Jack to consider FSU. Jack recently
remarked that he was highly impressed with Coach Pete's enthusiasm for
Florida State football. Jack also shared Coach Pete's dream of the Seminoles
developing into a national power in collegiate sports.

As a starting lineman at FSU in 1963, Jack made an immediate impact
on the team as a strong and aggressive middle guard. He was the starting
middle guard for three consecutive seasons from 1963 to 1965. Jack is now
forever linked to the stellar athletes who made up the FSU 1964 defensive
line, nicknamed the Magnificent Seven, sometimes called the Seven Magnificents, who will be further highlighted in a subsequent chapter in the
book. For now, to the younger FSU fans who may not know a lot about

Jack Shinholser, let me enlighten you. Jack was an imposing figure. He was about 6 feet tall, and weighed around 210 pounds. Jack was very muscular and was incredibly strong for his size. His teammates nicknamed him "The Wrecker" because of his ferocious style of play on the defensive line in the middle guard position.

As a young teenager still in high school and future FSU linebacker myself, I remember going to FSU games in Tallahassee on "recruit day" during the 1964 season. I was sponsored by another great FSU player from my home town named Del Williams, an All-American offensive guard for the Seminoles. I was fortunate to briefly see, or meet, some of the FSU football players, two of whom I near idolized at the time: Dick Hermann and Jack Shinholser. I distinctly remember noticing Jack Shinholser was very muscular, like a body builder. His arms reminded me of Popeye the Sailor, but Jack was certainly no joke. Jack had on his "game face," so I just kept quiet and avoided eye contact, hoping he wouldn't notice me. I must admit I was a little intimidated, mingled with awe, at the time. That day, I also remember closely watching both Jack and Dick Hermann in a now much-heralded game against in-state rival Florida in 1964. I was so impressed with both Jack and Dick. I recall how relentless and dominant they were on that great fall day in 1964 when we beat the Florida Gators for the first time.

COACH'S COMMENT "Coach Harbison built the 50-defense around a great nose tackle and Jack was that guy. He was likely our MVP on the 1964 team for his play at nose tackle. He was hard to block and could shoot the gaps. Very quick and a vicious hitter!" — Coach Bowden

As a big fan and highly interested observer, Jack always seemed to be performing at a higher level of self-discipline, quickness, and aggression than the opposing players. This was particularly true against rival teams and in critical moments in the game. Jack had the innate strength and ability to bull rush opposing linemen, shed their attempted blocks, and throw them aside like they were storefront mannequins being discarded or thrown in the air like confetti.

As an illustration, during the 1964 season, Jack is credited with causing a very timely fumble against the Florida Gators inside the Florida State five-yard line as Florida was threatening to score. Jack's quick and aggressive bull rush created havoc along the line of scrimmage, causing a traffic jam and a fumble, all at the same time. A study of the game film by FSU coaches the next day revealed Shinholser was somewhat of a hero, as time after time he drove the Gators' center into the Florida backfield and consistently pressured Florida's quarterback, the notorious Steve Spurrier. The fumble Jack caused on the 5-yard line effectively dashed the hopes of the Gators winning the game. Due to his stellar performance in this game, Jack was named National Lineman of the Week.

In a subsequent post-season game against Oklahoma in the Gator Bowl, Jack was once again honored as the Gator Bowl's Most Outstanding Lineman. At the close of his senior season, Jack was recognized by the Newspaper Enterprise Association (NEA) as a second team All-American and honorable mention All-American by AP and UPI. Playboy Magazine also named him a pre-season All-American. Jack Shinholser "The Wrecker" was truly an all-time Seminole great, one of the best ever to wear the garnet and gold.

In 2007, Jack was honored by being inducted into the FSU Athletic Hall of Fame, and the following is the citation for his selection:

> Jack Shinholser was an all-city, all-state and honorable mention All-American linebacker at Chamberlain High in Tampa, FL in 1961.
>
> Shinholser took a dominant role on the Seminole line as a sophomore in 1962. Although undersized at 208 pounds, he more than held his own and quickly earned a reputation as a ferocious player.
>
> Shinholser was credited with possibly the biggest defensive play of the 1964 season when he caused a Florida fumble inside the FSU 5-yard line that killed the Gator drive. He went on to be named National Lineman of the Week for his performance against the

Gators and was later the Outstanding Lineman of the 1964 Gator Bowl. He ranked third in tackles as a senior and was named Playboy Magazine Pre-season All-American and earned second-team All-American honors from the Newspaper Enterprises Association and honorable mention from both the Associated Press and UPI in 1964.

The Wrecker" as he was called by his teammates was drafted in the ninth round by the Washington Redskins and later by the Oakland Raiders in the AFL.

Following graduation from FSU, Jack played professionally for the Washington Redskins and Oakland Raiders. He then pursued his passion as a publisher and songwriter in the country music industry while also working full-time as a real estate management professional in Nashville, Tennessee. A successful real estate professional for most of his life, Jack is now fully retired. Jack and his wife, Verma, now reside in DeBary, Florida.

Winfred Bailey - Defensive Back 1961-1964

CHAPTER 9
MR. CLUTCH

John B. Crowe

Winfred L. Bailey came to Tallahassee as a highly recruited athlete out of Atlanta, Georgia in the fall of 1961. He was one of Coach Bill Peterson's key recruits in his first full recruiting class. Seminole fans sensed the beginning of an exciting brand of football in Tallahassee following the introductory year of Coach Pete's pro-style offensive football. All the FSU coaches needed to make the system go were the athletes. They would get a great boost with the incoming class that year. The 1961 recruiting class also included Jack Edwards, Bill "Red" Dawson, Jack Shinholser, Avery Sumner, Ed Pritchett, Steve Tensi, and Fred Biletnikoff. In Dr. Jones' book, "FSU One Time," he described this group as the material of greatness, and they delivered in 1964! Winfred would play a key role in the success in 1964. He always seemed to make a big play when the defense needed a stop. Winfred would intercept seven passes that year and was a member of the famed "Forgotten Four." He was a clutch player!

Winfred Leon Bailey was the 11th of 12 children: six boys and six girls. He grew up with four very aggressive sisters who toughened him up for sports and for life. All five brothers eventually served in the military. Winfred is very proud of all of his siblings. He grew up in Atlanta where there was a lot to do. His father worked as a night watchman and was a maintenance worker during the days. Watching his father and mother, Winfred grew up with a strong work ethic. His dad worked all the time and his mother stayed home and made sure he stayed out of trouble and went to church. Winfred remembers, "Mom and Dad taught us to be kind and to love each other." His brothers were mostly grown and gone, and he credits his sisters for his love for competition. He loved sports from an early age and was encouraged by his family to get involved. The Bailey home was near Georgia Tech's campus, and Winfred used this opportunity to sneak into Grant Field and watch Georgia Tech play football — he never got caught!

He dreamed of being a college football player and excelled at high school football, baseball, and track. He attended O'Keefe High School and was selected for many awards, including the Georgia All-State Football Team in both his junior and senior years. He won the Tom McCan Football MVP for Atlanta Schools in 1960. Winfred credits his teachers for building a desire to learn, and he developed good study habits while in high school that helped him succeed when he got to FSU. Winfred knew that his family wouldn't be able to provide the funds for college, and he knew his best opportunity would be an athletic scholarship. As an Atlanta high school star football player, he received attention from many colleges, but he was most impressed with Florida State and their new head coach, Bill Peterson. Winfred got a lot of attention from Coach Peterson and his staff, but the two individuals that sealed the deal were Dean Coyle Moore and a local FSU Alumnus, Howard Womack. Dean Moore was Winfred's role model and mentor. Dean Moore and his wife had a lifetime friendship with Winfred and his family.

Winfred came to FSU in the fall of 1961, and was a member of a very special class. He is very proud of being given the opportunity to be on the 1964 Seminole team, the team that put FSU on the national scene and is certainly a reflection point in Seminole Football history. That team had many firsts: first major bowl game and win, first Seminole team to defeat the Gators, first time FSU would crack into the AP Top 10 National Rankings, and the first team to have a consensus All-American — Fred Biletnikoff. While the offensive performances of wide receiver Biletnikoff and quarterback Steve Tensi are well known to college football fans, the defense that year gave up only 66 points in 10 regular season games and was key to one of the biggest upsets ever in college football. The Kentucky Wildcats, ranked No. 5, came to Doak Campbell Stadium on October 10, 1964, favored by three to four touchdowns. The final score that day would shock the nation and have one sports announcer declaring the report a mistake, saying "this must be backwards," with FSU 48 and Kentucky 6.

The defensive team that year became legendary. The defensive front seven were known as "The Seven Magnificents" and the defensive backs adopted the name "The Forgotten Four." Kentucky's only points came when they recovered a fumbled punt inside the six-yard line. If not for the fumble, "The Seven Magnificents and the Forgotten Four" would have delivered four shutouts in the first four games on their schedule. Winfred had an interception off the Kentucky quarterback and All-American, Rick Norton. Coach Peterson praised FSU's defense and said, "I think Winfred Bailey played the finest game I have ever seen a defensive back play."

The 1964 season would continue to be one to remember. Winfred intercepted a pass in seven out of 10 regular season games and made several key tackles to preserve wins in the Georgia and Florida games. He became known for coming through when the team needed a big play! His interception of a Steve Spurrier pass preserved the first ever win over the Florida Gators! He made seven of his team's 11 interceptions that year, and his total ranked him third in the nation. Winfred was selected to be a part of the first All-State College Football team in 1964, along with five other members of "The Seven Magnificents and the Forgotten Four."

COACH'S COMMENT   "Solid football player, versatile and smart!" — Coach Bowden

The 1964 team put Florida State football on the national stage and became one of the very special teams in FSU Football history! I would credit the 1964 team and the exciting football season that year for starting what would become a more balanced recruiting war for the top athletes in the South, and for making FSU competitive with Miami and the University of Florida. Seven members of the 1964 team are included in the FSU Athletic

Hall of Fame along with Winfred: Fred Biletnikoff, Steve Tensi, Bill "Red" Dawson, Del Williams, Dick Hermann, and Jack Shinholser .

Here is the citation to the award for Winfred from the FSU Athletic Hall of Commitee:

> Elected into the FSU Hall of Fame in 1989 Winfred Bailey began his Florida State football career in 1961 as a highly recruited halfback, playing behind the great Fred Biletnikoff. By his junior year, Bailey, an outstanding two-way player, had made a name for himself at defensive back. Bailey's finest year was 1964, his senior season, when he intercepted a team-best seven passes and was also a leading punt and kickoff returner. That year his efforts helped lead Florida State to an 8-1-1 record and a victory over Oklahoma in the Gator Bowl. Although his overall statistics are impressive, Bailey's contributions were perhaps greater because of his unique ability to come up with the big plays. Several times during his career, Bailey produced game-saving plays that made him one of Florida State's best defensive backs. Still an active supporter of the FSU program, Bailey is a successful businessman in Atlanta.

On Thursday, May 10, 2018, I had a couple of special hours with Winfred and his wife, Joy, at their home on Lake Lanier. They met at Florida State in a meteorology classroom and jokingly claim, "Life has been stormy ever since." Later they would go out on a "blind" date. They married in 1963 and have three boys. When I asked Winfred what he valued most in life he said, "My personal faith and family!" Winfred and Joy are very proud of their boys: two of the boys are attorneys and one is a doctor. Winfred is a very humble person, and feels blessed to have had the opportunities that football provided and has special feelings for FSU. He was a good student and always went to class. He tutored many of his teammates. He knew he needed the education to be successful in life. He made the Dean's List often and graduated with a degree in Accounting and Business Administration. He credits many of his lifelong friendships from his time at FSU and has special memories of his teammates, fraternity brothers, and professors. One of his best friends is Ed "Charlie" Pritchett, a star on the 1963, 1964, and

1965 Teams. Ed was also from Atlanta and a very versatile athlete while at FSU, playing quarterback, running back, and punting!

Winfred had special comments about Coach Pete and his position coach, Don James. He said they took an interest in their players and really loved them. He credits Coach James for teaching him more than just football tactics. Coach James also taught him the importance of hard work, being a team player, playing fair, and never giving up. Winfred said, "Coach James absolutely influenced my life." After graduation, Winfred began his business career as an accountant with Ernst and Ernst in Atlanta. He later did accounting work for a highway construction company before starting several very successful business adventures. He and Charlie Pritchett started a successful marble construction business that they sold after 20 years. Winfred then built houses and developments in a partnership company, B&H (Bailey and Harrison), before finally retiring in 2008.

Winfred is truly a success story and son of the Greatest Generation. He used his competitive spirit, family values, and athletic skills to attend college and have a very productive and successful business career. He values his experiences at Florida State and continues to support FSU as an active alumnus and contributor. When asked what he would like to be remembered for, he said, "That I was kind, helpful, and had some business success that allowed us to share with others." That desire is consistent for a player that would come through on the field when you needed a big play. Winfred is still a big play person, still Mr. Clutch.

Today, Winfred enjoys golf, tennis, bird hunting, and reading. He loves to read, especially about history. He and Joy like to spend time in their North Carolina mountain home with no phones or television — just quiet! They stay there until they get cabin fever!

I left the interview very impressed with the Bailey family. On March 16, 2018, Winfred was in a very serious automobile accident. He and I had planned to meet on March 26, and when I called on March 23 to verify our schedule, Joy informed me of the accident and that Winfred had serious head injuries and was in critical condition. Several weeks went by before

Winfred called me on May 3 to apologize for not getting back to me. He said that he would like to reschedule our interview. What I found on May 10 when I arrived at Winfred's and Joy's home was a miracle. His doctors were amazed that Winfred survived the accident. Winfred and Joy have a strong faith, and Winfred said, "I am living proof there is a protective and loving Heavenly Father. The Lord must have something else for me to do. It was not my time!" Joy is dedicated to being his caregiver during this period of recovery. Winfred is in therapy for his head injuries, and he knows that he has a way to go for full recovery. His persistence and the never-quit attitude that he learned from Coach James make all the difference. With their faith and each other, I believe they will prevail and continue to provide help and care for others! Winfred and Joy are a great team, and they are in my prayers!

Johnny Crowe - Defensive Back 1965 - 1968

CHAPTER 10

ONE OF A KIND

Dale McCullers

As a co-author of this book and a fellow teammate of Johnny Crowe in four seasons of Florida State football, I speak with informed authority when I say that he was one of the best defensive safeties in Florida State football history. Simply put, John B. "Johnny" Crowe is an American success story in the truest sense.

During his formative years, Johnny was reared in a hard-working, middle class neighborhood in St. Cloud, Florida. He attended St. Cloud High School where he excelled in both athletics and academics and graduated at the top of his class. Heavily recruited by FSU in his junior and senior year in high school, Johnny came to FSU as a football, basketball, baseball, and track star. Johnny continued to excel at FSU as both a highly driven scholar and very talented athlete. To Johnny's fellow athletes, considering his bright mind and superb football acumen, having Johnny on the field was like having a defensive coordinator on the football field during the game. As a defensive safety, Johnny functioned much like a combat field general. He expertly diagnosed plays, called defensive signals and audibles, completed sure and ferocious tackles at full speed, intercepted passes, and caused and recovered fumbles. In almost every game, he made big plays at critical moments. His confidence and passion for the game were contagious. In his senior season alone, he made an amazing 104 tackles and five interceptions and recovered three fumbles, unprecedented statistics for a safety.

I have already mentioned that Johnny was a ferocious hitter. As a former college and professional football player myself, I have never seen any defensive player, college or pro, make the kind of ferocious hits that Johnny made on ball carriers. Well, maybe one. I saw Dick Butkus once hit a running back so hard in a game against the Miami Dolphins, I felt what I thought was a small earthquake tremor. But back to Johnny. He made sure tackles with reckless abandon, always at full speed. From his safety position, if a receiver caught a flat pass at the line of scrimmage or a running back broke through the defensive line, you could always count on Johnny as a second line of defense. It was as if Johnny had been shot out of a cannon or was an incoming ballistic missile. The sound of him hitting an opposing player was like a clap of thunder near where you might be standing on the field. As a former collegiate and pro football player, I have never seen, nor heard, the kind of gridiron collisions Johnny routinely created on the football field. Johnny was one of a kind.

COACH'S COMMENT "I loved Johnny because he needed coaching. He was a quick learner and liked to hit!" — Coach Wyant

In addition to his outstanding gridiron play at FSU, in his senior year he was chosen as an academic finalist for the Rhodes Scholarship. This is an astounding accomplishment considering his weekly practice schedule, plus the additional time away from his studies because of travel and playing in games. In 1991, Johnny was inducted into the FSU Athletic Hall of Fame because of his outstanding career at FSU as a defensive safety. Included is the citation by the FSU Athletic Hall of Fame Committee:

When John Crowe came to Florida State in the fall of 1965, he came as a football, baseball, basketball, and track star. He also came as the top student from his high school class, with a 3.9 cumulative average. During his years with Florida State, he further developed his outstanding athletic and academic abilities, quarterbacking the defensive secondary and leading the way in the classroom. A big play man, Crowe was one of the hardest hitters on the team and was acclaimed the best safety in Florida State history. His junior and senior years with the Tribe, John did his best to live up to that accolade. His junior year he recovered a fumble in the Texas A&M game to set up the winning touchdown, leading Florida State to its first victory of the season. He finished his senior year with 104 total tackles, an incredible total for a defensive back, and five interceptions. John Crowe's hard-hitting style started a Florida State tradition of producing some of the hardest hitting safeties in the game.

In 1969, after earning a bachelor's and master's degree in mathematics at FSU, Johnny continued to excel in his professional career. His senior executive level experience and accomplishments after departing FSU are simply outstanding. John completed 26 years in the U.S. Air Force and served as a senior pilot before retiring from the military as a Lt. Colonel. He is also a Vietnam veteran who routinely flew over combat zones. In addition to his commendable military career, Johnny has over 33 years' experience in the forestry products industry at the senior executive level. As a former chairman of the board and CEO of Buckeye Technologies, he led the company to exceptional, profitable growth and stock appreciation. In 2013, Johnny also led the company into a very successful merger with Georgia Pacific.

COACH'S COMMENT   "Practiced like he played: always hustling and full speed ahead." — Coach Bowden

The rest of Johnny's personal involvement in state and local community causes, noteworthy charities, monetary endowments, and service on various national boards reads like a "Who's Who" American biography. Throughout the past 50 years, Johnny and his wife, Betty, have remained exceptional FSU alumni. In 2010, Johnny and Betty provided the FSU Mathematics and Athletic Departments a major gift to fund both athletic and academic programs in the form of arts and science activities and football scholarships for future Seminole football players. John and Betty are also active in, and provide service and/or monetary support to, many executive boards, trade associations, and local and national service/charitable organizations such as the United Way and the National Civil Rights Museum. To this day, John and Betty continually give their time, talent, and financial success, all for the benefit of others. Their philanthropy is truly legendary.

Walt Sumner - Defensive Back 1965 - 1968

CHAPTER 11

A Quiet Unassuming Cornerback

Dale McCullers

Many younger readers may not know Walt H. Sumner, but his was a household name in Southern Georgia. A native of Ocilla (Irwin County), Georgia, Walt is forever linked to some of the most exciting moments in Florida State football history. As a punt returner, defensive cornerback, and exceptional FSU baseball player, Walt is one of the greatest all-purpose athletes ever to don a garnet and gold jersey. Highlights of his college and professional football careers are a living testament of this remarkable and durable athlete. Walt always performed brilliantly in his role as a cornerback, but he played as if he was a stealth bomber, without fanfare or undue showmanship. Throughout the years, Walt has remained a quiet and reserved southern gentleman.

Walt was an exceptional two-way starter in high school as a quarterback and defensive back. He could have successfully competed for a chance to be a starting quarterback for the Seminoles, but he was asked by the FSU coaching staff to play defense early in his collegiate career. His defensive teammates were very fortunate to have Walt on their side of the field. While he was playing defensive football at FSU, Walt's demeanor and style of play was like a Bengal tiger patiently approaching and attacking its prey. Walt possessed razor-sharp football instincts. He roamed the field from his cornerback position with exceptional speed and precision. He could accelerate at full speed, whether on the football field or baseball diamond, and then stop on the proverbial dime. Walt also possessed a bright and incisive mind. He seemed to quietly diagnose and counter opposing players' tendencies and athletic moves with relative ease. As a former teammate and close observer, Walt never seemed to be out of position to make the big play in critical moments in the game.

COACH'S COMMENT
"I recruited and signed Walt. He was fast and had the quickness to be a great cornerback — and he was!"
— Coach Bowden

As a defensive player who also routinely blocked kicks and returned punts, Walt was true poetry in motion while serving on special teams. In the now-legendary tied game (37-37) against a No. 1 ranked Alabama team, Walt returned a punt 75 yards for a touchdown. Pandemonium erupted on both sidelines, and on live television, famed Alabama head coach Paul "Bear" Bryant was overheard to exclaim loudly, "What the hell is going on?" Let me tell you what was going on, folks. Walt was expertly following his defensive teammates' lead, who had built a man-made wall along the Alabama sideline, right in front of Coach Bryant. We practiced this special team play all week, and to our surprise, it worked beautifully. Our "perfect practice makes perfect" team motto paid off. Our combined efforts allowed Walt to prance into the end zone untouched. I might add it was Walt's full-speed decisiveness that made it work so well.

Such are the wonderful memories of a superb athlete named Walt Sumner.

COACH'S COMMENT
"Very quiet, but got it done and didn't say two words about it! Great quickness and great athlete. Didn't display emotions. Good coverage corner and sure tackler." — Coach Wyant

As a former teammate who knew Walt well, I can say with authority he was one of the best college athletes in the nation. Walt was a starting cornerback for three consecutive seasons at FSU, from 1966 to 1968. As a teammate, Walt was also a great role model. He possessed self-discipline, an even temperament, and an air of confidence. He was a true southern gentleman. I never heard anyone make a disparaging comment about Walt Sumner. The whole team would come to his defense if anyone did.

In 1982, due to his leadership on the field and stellar performance at FSU, Walt was elected into the FSU Athletic Hall of Fame. Included is the citation for his selection:

> Walt Sumner, corner back and punt returner, was a defensive leader for Florida State from 1965 through 1968. In 1966 and 1968 he led the squad in interceptions and in '68 he was tops in punt returns. In 1967, his 75-yard TD punt return against Alabama caused Coach "Bear" Bryant to exclaim on national television, "What the hell is going on?" In game after game, Sumner made key interceptions and used his speed to block kicks. After graduation, Sumner was a starter in the NFL, playing for the five years, 1969-1974, for the Cleveland Browns.

> At FSU, Walt Sumner was a two-sport athlete. On the diamond he played the outfield and in his senior year hit .300 while leading the Tribe in runs, doubles, and total bases.

> As a defensive back and an outfielder, this two-sport star ably represented Florida State University.

In addition to his legendary punt return against Alabama, Walt led the Seminoles in total interceptions and blocked kicks during his college career. Walt had a remarkable six blocked kicks as a Seminole. Following his senior year, the Cleveland Browns drafted Walt. He played six seasons for the NFL Browns, from 1969 to 1974, and made 15 interceptions and many exciting punt returns along the way. Walt Sumner was truly an all-time garnet and gold top performer.

Walt and his wife, Sandra, still reside in Ocilla, Georgia, their cherished hometown. Walt and Sandra were high school sweethearts. Walt was a star athlete, and Sandra was a cheerleader. Walt is a very successful CPA, and his wife Sandra is a middle school teacher. Neither plan to retire anytime soon. Walt and Sandra are active in their local church and other private business ventures. They remain ardent FSU fans and supporters.

Dale McCullers - Linebacker 1965 - 1968

CHAPTER 12

A Quiet Leader and the Assassin

John B. Crowe

I 've never met a young man from Live Oak who wasn't tough, and that includes Dale McCullers! Although a mild-mannered gentleman and unassuming person, Dale would strike his own mother if she were carrying a football. He roamed the football field like an assassin waiting to strike. Playing with Dale on the defensive team at Florida State from 1966 to 1968, it was difficult to make a solo or individual tackle because, more often than not, Dale was already making a hit on the opposing team's ball carrier, and the best you could do was add to the collision and get credit for an assist. Dale is one of the greatest linebackers to ever play at Florida State University and went on to be a great success in life. His total tackles during his junior and senior year, 180 and 163 respectively, were an amazing total. Dale roamed from sideline to sideline, and his instinct for getting to the ball carrier was special. You had the feeling that Dale knew the play. His position coach, Bobby Jackson, said, "I didn't need to over-coach Dale. [I] just lined him up and told him to go to the football, which he did and when he got there, he was usually in a bad mood." Given his performance in the 1968 season, Dale was named to the First Team NEA and Third Team AP All-American Teams.

COACH'S COMMENT   "Another tough athlete from Live Oak similar to Del Williams." — Coach Bowden

Dale would tell you that his early years in life were difficult. He was born in 1947 in Lake City, Florida, but he grew up in Live Oak. His father was a U.S. Army officer, and his mother was a housewife. Dale's parents divorced when he was only 5 years old. Dale's formative years were impacted by only brief exposure to both parents, as his father transferred to Germany and remarried while his mother suffered from mental illness and was in and out of hospitals. His mother didn't see Dale play football until the FSU-Memphis game in 1967 when the game was televised nationwide. Dale had an exceptional game, receiving recognition as National Lineman of the Week for his 17 unassisted tackles that day, including sacking the Memphis quarterback six times for a loss, which is still a Seminole one-game record. His mother phoned to tell him how well he played and how proud she was of him. Dale cherishes that phone call and memory. Dale was raised by his grandparents, Oscar and Annie Green, and bears their name: Dale Green McCullers.

In high school, Dale was an average student, tall and lanky in his youth. He developed a strong work ethic early in life working in the tobacco fields to earn money to buy his school clothes. Without a father figure around, coaches and teachers became his role models and mentors. Dale played both defense and offense in high school and excelled as linebacker for the Suwannee High School Bulldogs. It was in his junior year that he met the love of his life, Nell Evans. They dated throughout high school and were married after his senior year in college. They have now been married over 50 years.

Dale claims he was a late bloomer. I first met him when both of us came to Florida State University in the fall of 1965 on football scholarships. From the beginning, Dale was a leader. Though he was quiet, he led by example. He was a one-man wrecking crew. Dale came of age in the 1967 season. I was more intimidated by Dale and another teammate and linebacker named Mike Blatt over any offensive player I ever lined up against. Dale would get in your face if he thought you were performing at less than full speed. You didn't want to disappoint Dale! Dale had many great moments as linebacker and was recognized twice as National Lineman of the Week for the performance against Memphis, mentioned previously, and for his record performance against Texas A&M in 1968, making 29 tackles, which is still an FSU record.

Dale turned in a great performance against the Florida Gators in the first-ever Florida State win in "the Swamp" in 1967. Dale's style made playing my position as free safety easy in those years because he usually was on the ball carrier, or at least had cleared the path by taking out the blockers. Dale completed a very successful career at Florida State University with many records, including a 74-yard pass interception return against Houston. He was selected for the College All-American Bowl game in Tampa in 1969, in which he both started and starred.

If you check FSU's record book for defensive performance, you will see some amazing numbers for Dale. His numbers have stood the test of time, and even after 50 years of some great linebackers, he is near the top of the leader board! Dale's 180 tackles in the 1967 season is one short of Aaron Carter's 181 in 1977, placing him at second place on the all-time list. His total career tackles of 343 is 11th best in Florida State history and is an average of over 13 tackles per game played. Truly a remarkable Case for the Defense!

COACH'S COMMENT   "Very physical and tough. He would track down the football and make the hit! He would get to the action and make a difference. Hard to block." — Coach Wyant

Dale was selected in the draft his senior year by the Miami Dolphins and was later traded to the Baltimore Colts, where he was a part of the Super Bowl Five Championship Team in 1971, beating the Dallas Cowboys 16-13. Dale backed up two all-pro linebackers: Nick Buoniconti at Miami and Mike Curtis at Baltimore. That is pretty good company! Dale also played on the specialty teams. He decided after several concussions that he would leave pro football to pursue another career. Dale was inducted into the Florida State University Athletic Hall of Fame in the class of 1984, the first linebacker recognized by the Athletic Hall of Fame Committee. The citation for this honor states:

> From 1966 through 1968 a 198-pound linebacker from Live Oak, Dale McCullers, blazed his way into Seminole grid annals as one of the most brilliant defenders to play for Florida State. He led FSU defenders into three consecutive bowls: Sun, Gator, and Peach. In 1967, Dale was named AP lineman of the week after making 17 unassisted tackles against Memphis State. The following year AP honored McCullers again after he made 21 unassisted tackles in the Texas A&M game. He was the defensive leader in the '67 victory over Florida. At the close of his senior season Dale McCullers was chosen 1st team All-American by NEA and 3rd team All-American by AP. He was on AP's All-Southeastern Independent squad and played in the postseason All-American bowl. Quick, aggressive, and intelligent, Dale McCullers was truly an all-time garnet and gold football player.

Dale was always a role model for me and was certainly a credit to Florida State University. Football was a learning experience for Dale. He used the skills he gained from playing football as the bedrock of his life's foundation. He was, and is, more than a football player. He is a son of the Greatest Generation who has gone on to become an outstanding husband, father, criminology professional, and a great person. In Isaiah 30:15, it says, "Your strength will come from quiet confidence." Quiet confidence is an appropriate description of Dale McCullers.

Where is he now? In addition to his outstanding performance each weekend representing Florida State University, Dale eventually developed into a good student (Nell must have been the positive influence) and graduated with a bachelor's degree in criminology in 1969. His degree would serve him well! After departing from pro football, he began a career as a Criminal Investigator for the State Attorney, Third Judicial Circuit, in Live Oak, FL, from 1973 to 1977, followed by 23 years as a Special Agent in the Navy

Criminal Investigation Service (NCIS). Dale served in the United States and abroad, rising in rank to become a Senior Special Agent and Resident Agent at the Naval Air Station in Atlanta, Georgia. He later served as Senior Instructor at the NCIS Training Academy at the Federal Law Enforcement Training Center in Brunswick, Georgia. Dale retired from NCIS in 2003 and worked three years with Department of Homeland Security as Senior Instructor in Physical Technique Division before fully retiring in 2006.

Dale has served as a law enforcement consultant and taught criminology courses at Valdosta State, Okefenokee Tech, and Coastal Georgia College. For many years, he was an active motivational speaker for the Fellowship of Christian Athletes and other Christian groups. He also remains involved in local community affairs and humanitarian events. Dale and Nell have four children and seven grandchildren and currently live in Waycross, Georgia.

T.K. Wetherell - Defensive Back 1963-1967

CHAPTER 13

MR. SPEAKER AND MR. PRESIDENT

John B Crowe

Known as "T.K." by all of his friends and colleagues, Thomas Kent Wetherell came to Florida State University on a football scholarship in 1963. He was a tough competitor on and off the football field and played offense and defense from 1963 to 1967. While a big play man with many highlights and memorable moments in his football career, it's what he accomplished outside of football that makes his one of the greatest success stories of anyone who has ever worn the garnet and gold. T.K. served FSU, the state of Florida, and many other educational institutions with commitment, purpose, and passion as an educator, political leader, and in his "dream job" as president of Florida State University.

Born on December 22, 1945, he was in the first wave of baby boomers. T.K.'s great-great-great grandfather literally washed ashore in Daytona Beach, Florida. The Wetherell family was moving by boat from Philadelphia to Miami when a storm washed them ashore where Daytona Beach is today. Granddaddy Wetherell decided this place was good enough for him, and so they settled right there in the sand and palmettos. T.K. grew up and attended high school in Daytona Beach, Florida. He came from what he calls a normal American family where the children obeyed and greatly respected their parents. T.K.'s father was his boyhood role model, along with John Wayne, and he demonstrated a strong work ethic that has served him well. His father joined the Army Air Corps and served during World War II, instilling in his sons a passion for service. When his dad spoke, you listened; when mother spoke, everybody obeyed. Mr. Wetherell advanced through the ranks at Sears and Roebuck and had a long and productive career developing the idea of Sears' revolving credit card program and other inventive marketing ideas. T.K.'s family was always doing things together including Friday night football and evening meals. They were a solid family unit that lived a daily life that was full of important values and strong faith!

Daytona is famous for the Daytona International Speedway and the annual Daytona 500 race. Another of T.K.'s heroes was, and still is, Richard Petty. That may be why T.K. was such a fast runner — he loved the speed of the race car. His first job was mowing lawns, but he was always looking for adventure. T.K. loved the beach, ocean, and fishing and found ways to turn that passion into money. He started a fishing guide business, and he and a friend sold smoked mullet in the parking lot of the Daytona Beach Speedway during big racing weekends and events. Always the innovative leader, T.K. had a gift of attracting people to his team and leading them forward. The man had a gift for turning mullet into money!

T.K. grew up playing sports, most notably baseball, football, and track. He didn't play high school football until his junior year because it interfered with his fishing business, but with his great speed, he became a star on the team. Both T.K. and his teammate, Bill Moremen[1], signed football scholarships after their senior season to play football at Florida State University. Together, they had two of the most exciting plays in FSU history.

It was not as an athlete, but as a student leader that T.K. first came to FSU campus. In the summer of 1962, he attended the American Legion Boys State program at Florida State, as he had recently been elected student body president at Mainland High School in Daytona Beach. T.K. credits

---

1. Bill Moremen was a fine athlete and tough running back, and he had many great moments for FSU, but more importantly, Bill was a great friend and respected coach and educator. He is gone but not forgotten.

his positive experience at Boys State for having an impact on his choice of college. Coincidentally, T.K. and an assistant coach named Bobby Bowden came to FSU the same year. Also on the 1963 team were Wayne Giardino, Larry Green, Kim Hammond, Wayne McDuffie, Charles Pennie, Johnnie Stephens, and Del Williams, who all became valuable members of the varsity team in later years and left their mark on FSU football. T.K. played both offense and defense on the freshman team in 1963. This would be the last year that players had to play both ways, as the rule would change in 1964 to allow unlimited substitution. The experience served him well. T.K. was redshirted in the 1964 season to preserve a year of eligibility for the future. However, practicing with the 1964 team was a great experience and gave T.K. time to develop his skills for the years ahead.

COACH'S COMMENT   "Couldn't have been happier that year they assigned him to me as a defensive back. He had speed like Walt to make our unit very strong at both corners. Likely one of the fastest two corners in the nation in 1967." — Coach Wyant

I first met T.K. as a teammate at Florida State University in 1965. I was a freshman that year, and T.K. was a role model for me. I rushed a fraternity at the end of my freshman year, and T.K. was the major reason I joined Phi Delta Theta, where he not only became a teammate, but a brother in the bond. He played wide receiver for the Seminoles that year with high expectations for another dominating team, building on the success of the 1964 season with FSU's first victory over the Florida Gators and an outstanding Gator Bowl victory over a perennial power, the Oklahoma Sooners.

The 1964 season was likely the team that positioned Florida State University's football program on the big stage of college football featuring Fred Biletnikoff, Steve Tensi and the famous defensive team known as "The Seven Magnificents and the Forgotten Four." Most all of the defensive standouts on the 1964 team would return, and, while the offense needed to rebuild following Tensi's and Biletnikoff's departure to pro football, T.K. was the next great receiver and flanker. He didn't disappoint the fans and used his fast feet to be part of two of the greatest plays in Seminole football history, both kickoff returns. The first came against the Kentucky Wildcats in 1965 in the first 100-yard play in Seminole football history.

The second return was almost identical but came against Miami on September 24, 1966. It was late in the second quarter, and Miami had just gone ahead 13-7. On the kickoff that followed, Bill Moremen took the ball on the Seminole six-yard-line and ran to about the 17th, where he abruptly stopped and threw the ball across the field on a lateral to T.K., who caught it and used his gifted speed to race down the sideline behind a wall of Seminole blockers for a 94-yard-touchdown play. The Seminoles went on to win the hard-fought game 23-20.

Coach Peterson had success bringing the pro formation passing game to college football, and 1966 was another year of great passing success with a talented group of receivers. Billy Cox, Lane Fenner,[2] Thurston Taylor, and a passing combo from the freshman team of Gary Pajcic and Ron Sellers joined T.K. as receivers. Sellers became one of the greatest receivers to ever play college football, if not the greatest! I was a receiver on that team, and Sellers is the reason both T.K. and I became defensive backs. Covering Ron at practice during the week made Saturday a walk in the park, so thanks Ron!

In the spring of 1966, T.K. was moved to defense and became an outstanding cornerback, pairing with Walt Sumner. I was fortunate to play free safety with them in 1967. With Chuck Eason as the strong safety position and coached by Gary Wyant, we became a solid unit and were known as the "Rat Pack." I believe we got the name because we were lean and aggressive, resembling a group of rats running around on the field. Coach Wyant was affectionately called "Daddy Rat." We had the two fastest cornerbacks in

---

2. Who can forget his controversial catch against the Gators? This 55-yard pass was thrown by the FSU Quarterback to Lane Fenner for what appeared to be the winning score with only seconds left on the clock. However, the referee called Lane Fenner out-of-bounds. It was a heartbreaking loss for FSU with a final score of 21-16! The Florida defensive back would later verify that Fenner had made a great catch.

college football that year. T.K. and Walt were always assigned to the stand-out opposing receivers like Dennis Holman at Alabama, Richard Trapp at Florida, and Elmo Wright at Houston. The 1967 team was special, with three standout games: FSU tied Alabama 37-37, FSU and Penn State were Gator Bowl Co-Champs with a score of 17-17, and the first victory over the Gators in the Swamp 21-16. T.K. had a great year, and you could depend on him to be in the right position. We were a well-coached and close-knit group. T.K. told me that he wished he had switched to defensive back earlier in his career.

T.K. was a good student, and because of his redshirt year, he graduated before the 1967 season. T.K. was a graduate student, which meant that according to NCAA rules at that time, he was ineligible to play in post-season games and had to miss the Gator Bowl game. I believe if T.K. had played in that game we would have won. That rule has since been changed. Coach Peterson knew this could be a possibility, so he had a plan with the academic advisor and T.K. to enroll in only one hour of studies the spring of 1967 and finish his degree a year later. When T.K. told his mom the plan, she traveled to Tallahassee to have a meeting with Coach Pete and explained that he had made a promise to get her son his degree, and she didn't care about one more football game. That was that!

T.K. was elected into the FSU Athletic Hall of Fame in 1991 and was se-lected for the prestigious Moore-Stone Award. Here is the summary from the citation that accompanied the award:

> One of the most exciting two-way performers for the Tribe from the mid to late '60s was T.K. Wetherell. As a sophomore, T.K. was the second leading receiver on the squad, hauling in 19 passes for 234 yards and a touchdown. He also returned five kickoffs for an-other 194 yards. His junior year, Wetherell had a touchdown-kick-off return against Miami that was one of the highlights of the '66 season. It was the second time he and Bill Moremen had pulled the lateral play resulting in a kickoff return for a touchdown. He also had a touchdown reception against Wyoming in the Sun Bowl. That year, he caught 16 passes for 215 yards, returned one punt for

36 yards. On defense, T.K. finished out his senior season with the Seminoles with three interceptions for 65 yards and 10 punt returns for 18 yards. Today, he continues to serve Florida State as an avid fan and booster. He also represents his current alma mater well on the state level as he is the current speaker of the state of Florida House of Representatives. T.K. Wetherell's accomplishments both on and off the field make him an outstanding member of Florida State's Hall of fame and recipient of the prestigious Moore-Stone Award.

T.K. was much more than a football player. After graduating from FSU with bachelor's and master's degrees, he received his Ph.D. in 1974 in Education Administration. He has made significant contributions in his career in education, including serving as provost and vice president of Daytona Beach Community College, president of the Independent Colleges and Universities of Florida, and president of Tallahassee Community College. In addition to education, he served as an elected public official. He was first elected to the Florida House of Representatives in 1980 and reelected several times thereafter. In 1991 and 1992, he was elected Speaker of the House of Representatives. He was devoted to both careers and put time and energy into improving state education at all levels. His journey is special and likely at the top of his accomplished career is what he calls his "dream job": president of Florida State University. T.K. served FSU as President from January 6, 2003 to January 31, 2010, and during that time, Florida State University made great strides and received national recognition. The changes and accomplishments are many. When I asked T.K. what stands out as his most important contribution and what he would want for a legacy, he replied, "I would like to be remembered for making a positive difference and for always being willing to help make things better." What a great career!

COACH'S
COMMENT   "Great athletic ability and could still be an impact player today." — Coach Bowden

Thomas Kent Wetherell made a positive difference wherever he was. I have watched his amazing career, knowing that he was also battling stage four cancer, beginning in 2002. T.K. and his wife, Ginger, fought with determination and courage while at the same time serving as President and First Lady of FSU. Ginger is a great success story by herself!

T.K. loved to hunt and fish as a youngster and still does today, demonstrating his passion for the outdoors. Maintaining two spectacular properties in Florida and Montana, T.K. and Ginger love to drive their tractors and other equipment as they preserve the forest and land with Mother Nature. The example they set is moving and inspiring. Their testimony is one of faith, hope, and love, and they live it — one day at a time! I am proud to be a friend of T.K.

Thomas Kent "T.K." Wetherell passed away on Sunday, December 16, 2018. His courageous battle with cancer is over — he was a warrior to the end. I sat with him on December 7th and read his chapter to him. He approved and claimed I made him sound better than he was. I would respectfully disagree. Dale and I, along with our teammates, have lost a remarkable friend. His passion for FSU and what he did to improve the University are special. I personally feel like I have lost a brother. T.K. is gone, but never forgotten.

J.T. Thomas - Defensive Back 1969-1972

CHAPTER 14
THE TRAIL BLAZER

John B. Crowe

J.T. Thomas attended Lanier High School in Macon, Georgia and came to Florida State University in 1969. In 1970, J.T. became one of the first African American football players to play at FSU. Soon thereafter, in the 1970 season, two other African American players, Charlie Hunt and Eddie McMillan, joined J.T. in the starting lineup. All three went on to star on defense, all while breaking down racial barriers.

After an amazing career at FSU, J.T. was honored with an All-American selection his senior year. He received an honorable mention for All-American status his sophomore and junior years at FSU. J.T. Thomas had many firsts while at FSU and was truly a trailblazer, making a strong Case for the Defense!

After playing at Florida State, J.T. was the Steelers' first-round selection (24th overall) in the 1973 NFL draft. He was FSU's first defensive player selected in the first round. That year, Thomas played in all 14 regular-season games and in the Steelers' only playoff game. He went on to play for the Steelers until 1981 and was a part of their famous "Steel Curtain" defense. He was selected for the Pro Bowl in 1976. J.T. was with the Steelers until 1982 before he moved to the Denver Broncos for one year, retiring from pro football in 1983. J.T. was a big play defensive back throughout his entire career, beginning with two blocked kicks in his first game at FSU and culminating in the fourth Super Bowl Championship he played in. He proudly wears four Super Bowl rings.

Growing up in the mid-1960s had its challenges. There was a lot of political uncertainty surrounding integration and the Civil Rights Movement; America's involvement in Vietnam; and challenges to conventional family values.

Macon, Georgia was no exception. James T. Thomas grew up in the middle of all of it. He wasn't initially interested in football or any sports, but wanted to focus on music and playing the piano. He attended an all-black private Catholic school, St. Peter Claver, which was staffed by Sisters of the Blessed Sacrament. James T. had a speech impediment as a young man, and the nuns hired him to do odd jobs at the convent primarily to work on this handicap, eventually correcting his ability to pronounce words. During lunchtime, he would get drilled on his pronunciation. J.T. recalls that even though his speaking ability improved, his status in his neighborhood didn't because he wasn't speaking like everyone else.

COACH'S COMMENT   "He was a freshman my last year at FSU, so I didn't get the chance to coach him, but he was a trail blazer for sure. He was a great one!" — Coach Wyant

J.T. was the oldest of four children, with two sisters and a younger brother 12 years his junior. His motivation for getting involved in football came from his decision to develop his physical skills and strength so he could confront his father for his abusive behavior with J.T.'s mother. J.T. had noticed his father used high school football players to lift cars onto blocks and install transmissions. He started watching the Green Bay Packer players, Herb Adderley and Willie Woods, two gifted and all-pro cornerbacks in the 1960s. He admired the way they could run backwards (backpedal is the term for the skill), and he started practicing the art. His mother would say, "What are you doing, trying to kill yourself?" When he told her he was going to play football, she told him that the white boys would kill him.

With his mind made up and his goal to stand up to his father, J.T. began developing his football skills at St. Peter Claver during recess and found he had the ability to catch the ball. He wanted to be a wide receiver.

In the mid-1960s the Civil Rights Act initiated the process of integration. James T. became a trailblazer for the efforts in Macon schools when Mother Superior Josepha recommended J.T. enroll at Lanier High School, becoming one of the first black students to attend the previously all-white school. J.T. entered the ninth grade at Lanier with a few other black students and remembers being escorted to and from the campus by the Highway Patrol.

He also remembers developing a process that he used throughout his football career of putting his jersey over his shoulder pads before putting on his pads. This was because the white players helped each other when pulling on the jersey, but that wasn't something he could count on. I could share many more stories of his trailblazing experiences. However, those stories will be better shared by J.T. as he is writing a book about his life with the tentative title "From the Balcony." In the book, he will look back on the past from a different angle. He reflects on things that happened to him and notices new things he didn't see as it was happening. His story is special; it is worth understanding what a young black male went through growing up and pursuing a high school and college education during this period in our history. J.T., like all of the players highlighted in our book, needed the football scholarship to afford college. While several schools believed it was too early to bring in black athletes, Florida State and Bill Peterson saw the talent in J.T. and offered him a football scholarship. We all should be thankful they did.

He was truly a trailblazer, an outstanding high school player, college All-American, and NFL All-Pro with the Pittsburgh Steelers. While his mother kept him on the straight and narrow with her Bible teachings and meaningful scriptures, J.T. never got to confront his father directly. Instead, his success at Lanier prompted a change in his father, and J.T. remembers the day his father told him that he gave his life to the Lord. J.T. came to FSU without any guidelines, instructions, or how-to's, but he persisted, becoming one of the first black athletes to step onto the playing field as a Seminole.

He shared with me the scripture verses that his mother would use to reinforce her guidance, including Philippians 4:6 and 4:13 and Hebrews 4:16. I read them, and the message is powerful. To summarize the power of her guidance, I have included Philippians 4:13: "I can do all things through him who strengthens me." J.T. went on to make an impact that will be forever important to FSU and led the way for other black athletes. He wore number 26 at FSU in honor of his early role model, a member of Pro Football Hall of Fame and All-Pro Green Bay Packer, Herb Adderley. They would later become friends. However, when he joined the Steelers the number 26 was already being worn by a great running back, Preston Pearson, so J.T. wore the number 24, which was Willie Wood's number with the Packers.

James T. Thomas's accomplishments are truly special. Like so many defensive backs, he came to FSU as a wide receiver, but became a defensive back. In 1979, he was inducted into the FSU Athletic Hall of Fame. I have included the citation for that recognition.

> One of Florida State's most brilliant defenders, James 'J.T.' Thomas began his Seminole career with a sensational performance and ended as an All-American. As one of FSU's first black football players,[3] Thomas blocked two field goals in his first game in 1970. That same year the Macon, Georgia, native tied the FSU record for single-game interceptions with three. In 1972, Thomas, who began his career as a cornerback and ended as a safety, was a first team All-American pick by Pro Football Weekly and Time Magazine. He

---

3. J.T. Thomas was one of the first black football players at FSU, but Calvin Patterson was the first black athlete to receive an FSU football scholarship in 1968, a year before Thomas. Calvin played on the freshmen team in 1968 and was on the varsity roster in 1969. Calvin Patterson's life ended tragically on August 16, 1972. For more about Calvin, readers should reference the article "Tragic story of Calvin Patterson: 1st black football player at FSU" by Mark Schlabach on ESPN.com. Both J.T. and Calvin were trail blazers!

went on to an outstanding professional career with the Pittsburgh Steelers winning four Super Bowl rings as a member of the famed 'Steel Curtain' defense.

There are numerous references to J.T.'s accomplished career. He has received many awards, including being a member of the Georgia Athletic Hall of Fame. I wanted to provide a brief summary of his accomplishments as a professional player. First, he was a first round draft pick of the Pittsburgh Steelers in the 1973 draft. In 1974 and 1975, the Steelers won back-to-back Super Bowls.

In 1974, Thomas had a career-best of five interceptions, and he scored a touchdown on a fumble recovery. Thomas was named to the Pro Bowl game after a 1976 season in which he collected two interceptions and a fumble recovery. During his time in Pittsburgh, Thomas played alongside cornerback Mel Blount. NFL.com named Thomas and Blount the sixth-best cornerback combination of all time. During the 1982 preseason, Thomas was traded to the Denver Broncos for a draft slot. J.T. played in four Super Bowls with the Steelers and has four championship rings.

J.T. retired from football in 1983 and began a career in the restaurant and food service industry. J.T. was always a good student and was the valedictorian at St. Peter Claver, developing his ability to focus and retain information. He graduated from FSU with a business degree and had an interest in real estate development. J.T. prepared and had plans that didn't depend on a football career. He has had successful ventures managing restaurants, beginning with a Chinese restaurant then became a franchisee of Burger King, Applebee's, and Red Hot & Blue Southern Grill. J.T. and former teammate Larry Brown owned, operated, and developed the Applebee's chain in the central and western Pennsylvania and Morgantown, West Virginia market for more than 20 years.

Currently, J.T. is a franchise owner of Crazy Mocha, a local coffee chain in the Pittsburgh market. While at FSU, he met and married Deborah just prior to graduation, and they have two children. They have helped raise many other children, including two daughters of his sister who passed away at an early age; they are currently raising two of their grandchildren: 17-year-old Jerrell and 11-year-old Nikira. Recently, I met with J.T. at the Crazy Mocha to discuss his current activities, and it was clear that he understands the food business, people, and is an entrepreneur.

The walls in the Crazy Mocha are filled with pictures of Steelers teammates and coaches and Pittsburgh jazz legends, like George Benson and Ahmad Jamal. What a great tradition and atmosphere!

Besides developing his business, he attends his grandchildren's sports and music activities. He also leads a weekly men's Bible study supported by his online scripture lessons. When asked what he would like to be remembered for, he said, "I have yet to arrive and have more to do. I want to continue to give and share myself with others, creating support and opportunities for them." He is still energized and discovering things about himself.

The Thomas family lives in Monroeville, Pennsylvania, a town just east of Pittsburgh, so J.T. remains active in both communities. He continues the work on his book in the little free time allowed by his many activities and believes life's events are connected. Looking back on the road he has traveled, he told me that he wouldn't change a thing or want to do anything over. He is a man of faith and has immense loyalty to his friends and family. He is thankful for his teammates and stays close to many of them, both college and professional. The day I met with him, he was wearing a ball hat with the following words inscribed on the front: "Man of Faith" and on the bill of the cap: "I Love Jesus."

I will always value the time I spent with James T. Thomas and found many of the same traits that I found in the interviews with the other men in this book: faith, a plan for life, persistence, family values, and a humble mental and physical toughness. James T. Thomas is a legend and role model. I sincerely hope he completes his book "From the Balcony." While the other men in our book had challenges to overcome, none faced the racial issues that he did. He has much to share, and I could not adequately represent all his experiences. FSU is blessed that J.T. Thomas came in 1969 and blazed a trail!

Lee and John reminiscing about FSU football!

Coach Peterson and Dale
sharing some stories at the
Tallahassee QB Club!

A catch made in the days before "play under review."

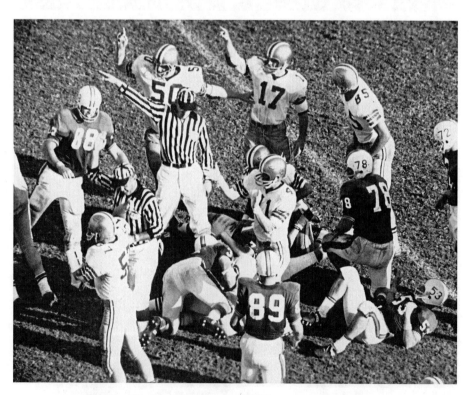

The fumble that sealed the first FSU victory in the Swamp.

A helmet that reminds us of "the way we were."

J.T. and John in the Crazy Mocha in Pittsburgh.

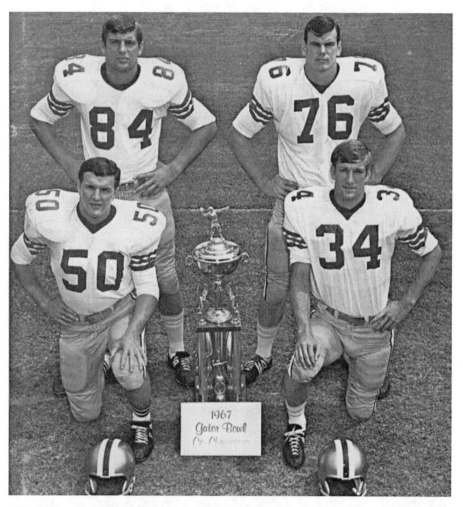

The 1968 team senior leaders and pro prospects: McCullers, Sellers, Glass, and Fenwick.

PART 2

COACHES' CORNER

DEFENSIVE COACHES AND FSU LEGENDS

This section of the book captures the comments of coaches that dedicated themselves to developing defensive football players.

Coaches Jackson, Wyant, and Harbison were defensive assistant coaches and developed the Sons of the Sixties, along with our head coach Bill Peterson. The 1960s are known as the Peterson Era.

Coaches Bowden, Gladden, and Andrews teamed together to deliver the Bowden Era and the remarkable Dynasty Years. Their distinguished coaching careers make a Case for the Defense, and they are also Sons of the Greatest Generation and Sons of the Sixties.

Coach Bobby Jackson - Linebackers 1965-1969

CHAPTER 15

BOBBY JACKSON – A PLAYER'S COACH

Dale McCullers

FSU ASSISTANT COACH — DEFENSIVE ENDS AND LINEBACKERS — 1965-1969

It is an esteemed honor to prepare this featured chapter about one of my favorite FSU coaches and superb mentor, Coach Robert "Bobby" Lanier Jackson. From a player's perspective, as one of many who knew him well, Coach Jackson was, and still is, an extraordinary man. In his younger days, he was a two-time small college All-American who played running back for the legendary FSU coach Bobby Bowden at South Georgia College and Howard College in Birmingham, Alabama.

Later, during his collegiate and professional coaching career, he clearly distinguished himself as a superb coach, mentor, motivator, and, on game day, a tactical leader of men. Coach Jackson served for almost two decades in various roles as an assistant coach or defensive coordinator at Florida State, Kansas State, Louisville, and Tennessee. He then spent an additional 21 years as an assistant coach or offensive coordinator for the Atlanta Falcons, San Diego Chargers, Phoenix Cardinals, Washington Redskins, St. Louis Rams, and the Miami Dolphins.

During each tour of duty in his illustrious career, he was viewed by players and coaches alike as an exceptional leader and dedicated coaching professional. In 1965, he came to FSU in the role of an unpaid graduate assistant coach for the Seminoles. In 1966, he began his official coaching career at FSU as a defensive end and linebacker coach. During the 1966, 1967, and 1968 football seasons, Coach Jackson was directly involved in my development as a college linebacker. First, he coached me as an unproven sophomore linebacker and then as a starting linebacker for the Seminoles my junior and senior year at FSU.

Speaking from my perspective as a former college and professional football player, I can best describe Coach Jackson as a charismatic leader and a truly gifted professional. The footprint of his remarkable life is clearly visible in his stellar coaching career. Personally, he has been a lifelong role model and someone I genuinely admire.

Coach Jackson possessed the unique ability and personality traits to make his position players feel like he was their personal coach, friend, and colleague. Coach Jackson made you feel appreciated and admired, both as a football player and as an individual. He also firmly established and maintained boundaries within the coach and player relationship. In my view, he was at his best as a defensive end and linebacker coach, but he was equally lauded throughout his career as a great quarterback and running back coach. And then, not to be labeled or limited as a position coach, he also flourished and distinguished himself in the college and professional ranks as a stellar offensive coordinator.

Coach Jackson was an equally exceptional sideline coach on game day. At FSU, he taught his position players the enabling power of hard work and self-confidence. In practice and during games, he fostered a strong work ethic and a true-grit style of play. He often emphasized the need for "mental toughness," and he inspired those whom he coached to perform at the highest level possible.

Coach Jackson often provided little golden nuggets of timely and expert advice, which really helped increase each player's competitive edge without "over-coaching." He had a way of settling the player down and reducing anxiety while still focusing on the job at hand. Another remarkable trait was his ability to develop the unique skill set of each player he coached and maximize those skills during fierce competition. He often provided animated demonstrations on how to neutralize or shed blocks and to get to the ball carrier to avoid taking a bad angle, or making bonehead mistakes by committing costly penalties.

Coach Jackson's keen understanding of the game, coupled with his exceptional knowledge of the X's and O's, led to many spontaneous tips for his team in critical moments of the game. Coach Jackson was an exceptional player himself; he knew what he was talking about and was not just whistling Dixie. His coaching and counsel were not guesswork. Coach Jackson was never demeaning and seemed to function more as an advocate than a critic. He could raise his voice, and his expression may have been sometimes very serious, but you knew he was in your corner, win, lose or tie. I remember Coach Jackson as a man who could "chew you out and make you like it, all at the same time."

His discerning eye routinely helped individual players read offensive tendencies and increase application of their God-given talents. I suppose developing and significantly increasing a player's known and hidden talents and becoming a better student of the game, was the genius behind his extraordinary success as a coach. His words and demeanor, often unbeknown to him, were the catalyst for many players developing into better athletes and better prepared teammates. Coach Jackson's players especially admired him when he lifted spirits and helped restore dignity after some very agonizing losses. In summary, Coach Jackson was a superior coach, a player's coach, and a fine Christian gentleman in the truest sense of the word.

Because of his unique skill set, he was a hot commodity as a coaching professional. His coaching resume and his long and successful career are living testaments of his value at the many universities and professional football teams that sought his services.

Coach Jackson's numerous accomplishments and the number of All-American's and All-Pro's he coached throughout his career are too numerous to list in this book. However, just a few of his more notable accomplishments and coach/player relationships are cited below:

- Declared to be "the best all-around player I ever coached" by legendary FSU Coach Bobby Bowden;

- Two-time small college All-American running back who ran for 27 touchdowns and 2084 yards, —a 7.3-yard average — in his collegiate career;

- Coached FSU All-American linebacker Dale McCullers, who later played professionally for the Miami Dolphins and Baltimore Colts;

- Coached multiple star running backs in his 21-year professional career who exceeded 1,000 yards rushing in a season under Coach Jackson's tutelage: Marion Butts and Gary Anderson for the San Diego Chargers; Ronald Moore for the Phoenix Cardinals; Terry Allen (twice) and Stephen Davis for the Washington Redskins; and NFL Hall of Fame running back Marshall Faulk (twice) for the St. Louis Rams.

Where is he now? Coach Jackson fully retired in 2007. He now resides in Alpine, Alabama with his wife Nancy. He raises cattle on his farm and is a motivational speaker, particularly in the area of sports and Christianity, as he is also very active in the Fellowship of Christian Athletes. He and his wife Nancy are also involved in community affairs and humanitarian activities.

IN HIS OWN WORDS
Coach Bobby Jackson

During my tenure as an FSU assistant coach, there were many exceptional Seminole football players I personally coached or indirectly coached during the 1965 to 1969 Seminole football seasons. In my opinion, all of these young men proudly wore the garnet and gold uniform on college game day. A few special players from an earlier decade, or some elite athletes from a yet future decade, may have possessed more raw talent or a greater work ethic, but as a whole, none seemed to be more united, more competitive, more hard-nosed, or more passionate than the players of the 1965 to 1969 era of Florida State Football.

Prior to my coaching debut at FSU, I was already a big fan of Seminole football. I also had a strong connection to FSU through legendary Coach Bobby Bowden, who coached me as a running back when Coach Bowden was the head coach at Howard (Samford) College in Birmingham, Alabama. In the early 1960s, Coach Bowden left Howard College to take an assistant coach position at FSU. In 1965, Coach Bowden was instrumental in helping me secure a position on the FSU coaching staff as a volunteer (non-paid) graduate assistant. As a fan of Seminole football and with my strong connection to coach Bowden, I was also very familiar with the notorious group of FSU defenders nicknamed "The Magnificent Seven." This stellar group of defensive linemen who played during the 1964 season helped bring nationwide attention and recognition of FSU as an emerging college football power. Unfortunately, I did not have the opportunity to coach any of these great Seminole defensive players, as I did not actually begin my coaching career at FSU until the 1965 season.

At this time, as both an avid fan and aspiring FSU coach, I recall the exceptional play of FSU's marquee linebacker Dick Hermann and Jack Shinholser, FSU's exceptional middle guard. Both were outstanding defensive players.

Dick graduated from FSU in 1964, prior to my arrival as a coach, and Jack played for the Seminoles through his senior year in 1965. However, as a graduate assistant coach at FSU during the 1965 season, I was not personally involved in Jack's collegiate career or development. I will say, both Dick Hermann and Jack Shinholser were clearly and unequivocally talented, hard-nosed players. All of the "Magnificent Seven" linemen, in my opinion, were an elite group of defensive players. From a coaching perspective, in Dick's assigned role as a linebacker, and in Jack's role as a middle guard, no tandem appeared to work more effectively together as these two did. These stand-out players both earned their high distinction as members of the FSU Athletic Hall of Fame.

During the 1966 to 1968 seasons, as a defensive end and linebacker coach, I was personally or indirectly involved in the collegiate careers of future FSU Athletic Hall of Fame players Dale McCullers, Walt Sumner, and Johnny Crowe. I also knew and admired FSU defensive back T.K. Wetherell, who was an exceptional athlete and worthy recipient of FSU's Moore Stone Award.

T.K.'s contributions to Florida State University as an exceptional athlete, student, and legendary FSU administrator are without parallel. All of these players were exceptional in their own unique way and truly deserve the recognition they have received. In my view, they all made major contributions to Florida State University as an elite group of football players. It is also clear that they were all successful in their respective post-college professional careers. I would like to add some comments on Walt, Johnny, and Dale individually.

Walt Sumner was an exceptional player. He was smooth and agile. He was somewhat reserved, but he possessed great athletic skill and was a great team player. He was exciting to watch in games and made many huge plays at critical moments in the game.

Johnny Crowe was highly intelligent and a hard worker; it was like having a coach on the field. He had a keen perception for diagnosing plays and making sure tackles. He was a superb student of the game and probably knew more than the coaches did.

Dale McCullers was as tough as 18 acres of garlic. He seemed to be on a mission while playing linebacker, and he was quick and aggressive. Just line him up and tell him to get to the ball carrier, and he did. Dale was the first All-American I had the privilege to coach in my career, so Dale will always be special to me.

Coach Gary Wyant - Defensive Backs 1966 - 1969

CHAPTER 16

GARY WYANT – "DADDY RAT"

John Crowe

oach Wyant can best be described as a perfectionist. He was willing to work long hours to make sure every detail was covered inside and out on every job or task he was given. He required total dedication from himself and held others to the same high standard. That was certainly his persona when he was the defensive back coach at Florida State University, coaching a group of undersized young men from 1967 to 1969. Not everyone could meet his standards, but those who did became a solid unit and team. Because of our size and our hustle — and the toughness that Coach Wyant developed in each of us — one Director of Sports Publicity named us the "Rat Pack." He once said, "Look at them out there, running around like a bunch of wild mice chasing after cheese." So we were known as the "Rat Pack" and even had our own logo, shirt, and jacket. Coach Wyant was affectionately known as "Daddy Rat."

The Rat Pack was always prepared, and while sometimes we would get outplayed, it was usually because of the opponents' skills and not lack of execution on our part. We wore out the projector watching films on our opponents. In 1967 through 1969, the Seminoles intercepted 63 passes, an incredible number that averaged out to over two picks per game. In 1968, the Seminoles led the nation with 25 interceptions.

Like the defensive players who have made a Case for the Defense, Coach Wyant was also a Son of the Sixties and came from parents of the Greatest Generation.

Gary Wyant was born in 1940, the only child of Dorothy Grace and Woodrow Wilson Wyant. His parents met in a poor rural farming community in Kansas, the same town they grew up in. Woodrow finished high school, and after marriage, decided to leave the farm. He initially worked for the Santa Fe Railroad before beginning training as a chiropractor. The family initially lived in Medicine Lodge, Kansas. Coach Wyant remembers moving many times as his dad looked for the ideal place to open his practice. One of those moves was to Oregon, and they spent some time traveling in the northwestern United States. Oregon law required Woodrow to take additional training before he could get a license to practice, so after much consideration, the family returned to Wichita, Kansas where he opened an office in their home. This would be the final move; Coach Wyant attended school in Wichita and developed his passion to coach.

Once his family settled in Wichita, Coach Wyant became active in sports, excelling in football, basketball, baseball, and track. In middle school, he played basketball and ran track but focused on football and baseball in high school. He attended Wichita East High, a very large school that had over 3,600 students. He played quarterback on the football team and all the infield positions in baseball, but preferred first base because of his admiration for Stan "The Man" Musial. He remembers listening to the St. Louis Cardinals broadcast during the seasons and recalls the commentary by Hall of Fame Pitcher Dizzy Dean and Buddy Blattner; Dizzy with his colloquialisms and mangling of the English language and Buddy for his description of what really happened.

Coach developed his work ethic as a young man working in the local flour mill. He shoveled out the wheat cars and recalls the long hours, poor breathing conditions, and the pay. It was a great job at that time — he made $2.65 per hour and had a lot of overtime. That meant Coach would work until there weren't any railcars of wheat on the site. Coach would work all summer, and he would look like a ghost every day when he came home. During school breaks, Coach also worked as a carpenter's assistant and worked with the city sewer construction crew. These were the types of jobs available in those days — there weren't many food service jobs like McDonald's, Wendy's, or Burger King. His working experiences made an impression and convinced Coach to pursue a college education. Seems to be a common theme for the Sons of the Sixties.

Lessons learned: Have a plan, become physically tough, and be persistent!

Because his high school had a large enrollment, it was difficult to make the varsity team until junior or senior year. Coach related an experience that changed his life during his senior year on the football team. Gary got a little out of step with his coach and was told to put all of his equipment and uniforms that belonged to the school in his locker and never come back. This was just before his team was to compete in the playoffs. After five days, Gary couldn't stay away and went to see his coach, Bob Shepler. Gary pleaded his regrets and apologized, but Coach Shepler wasn't buying it. Gary was really disappointed, but three days passed and Coach Shepler called him in and gave him another chance. Looking back, it would be the moment Gary decided he wanted to be a football coach. Coach Wyant remembers Coach Shepler with special appreciation and respect for making a difference in his life and being responsible for his career in coaching and the other successes he has had in life. Coach Wyant received a football scholarship at Wichita State following his senior season and credits Coach Shepler for preparing him to move to the next level.

Coach enrolled at Wichita State University in the fall of 1958 and went on to play half back and defensive back for the next four years. He became a defensive specialist during a period when the substitution rules allowed one sub, usually for the quarterback, at the change of possession. Coach would be that sub. Wichita State's head coach was Hank Foldberg and the Shockers won the Missouri Valley Conference in Coach Wyant's junior and senior years, 1960 and 1961. The Shockers had several memorable wins and this would start a trend of Coach Wyant being part of a winning team. He played in the 1961 Sun Bowl.

After graduation in 1962, Gary began his coaching career as the head fresh-man coach at Wichita State. Coach Wyant took the lessons he learned as a player, and later as a defensive back coach, to develop, lead, and prepare players and employees to achieve their potential in football, academics, and business.

Coach Wyant was a highly respected defensive back coach. Every program that he was associated with had winning seasons. He was a determined and motivated teacher and coach. He understood the fundamentals of being a defensive back and could teach and develop those skills in the young men he worked with at Wichita State, Florida State, University of Georgia, University of Tennessee, and Texas Tech University. He worked with many successful programs and head coaches that included Vince Dooley, Bill Battle, Phil Fulmer, Steve Sloan, Bill Peterson, Joe Gibbs, Bill Parcells, Dan Henning, and Rex Dockery, to name a few.

He came to FSU in 1966 as linebacker coach and moved to coaching de-fensive backs in 1967-1969. In 16 years as a college coach, he participated in 10 bowl games. Three of those games were while he was at FSU, the Sun and Gator Bowls and the first Peach Bowl.

When speaking with Coach Wyant, he recalled four milestone games at Florida State and could play back many of the key plays. First up was the 37-37 tie with Alabama in 1967. The Crimson Tide were the defending national champions in 1966 and had given up only 36 points that year. FSU's performance that day was amazing and even received great praise from Coach Paul "Bear" Bryant. Coach Wyant also could quickly review the Penn State and Florida games during the 1967 season and how the Seminoles shut down the Houston Cougars' high-powered offense in 1968!

Coach Wyant began making a career change in 1978 and decided that he wanted to settle down with his family. He chose to begin a career in banking and was given the opportunity by the family of a former player from the University of Tennessee. Coach started at the entry-level position and learned the banking business from the ground up. He moved with his wife, Betty, and their three children to Sparta, Tennessee. Sixteen years later, he was promoted to Vice President of the First National Bank of Sparta. When the bank became part of Dominion Bank and finally the First Union National Bank of Tennessee, he served as Senior Vice President and Vice President respectively. Always a good judge of character, he was responsible for personal and commercial loans, and you can bet the loans were made good!

In 1994, Coach Phil Fulmer became the head coach at the University of Tennessee and invited Coach Wyant to come back to athletics. Coach Fulmer wanted Coach Wyant to put his organizational and leadership skills to work as his Assistant Athletic Director for Football Operations. Coach Fulmer and Coach Wyant had coached together at the University of Tennessee during the early 1970s and had become close friends. Coach Wyant made the decision to return to athletics. He again rose to higher levels of responsibility. He worked with Athletic Director Doug Dickey to make significant contributions to the athletic programs at the University of Tennessee. He was a key leader in the improvement of athletic facilities for sports for both men and women, making the University of Tennessee one of the premier athletic programs in the nation. Coach Wyant retired as the Executive Associate Athletic Director in 2008. He is still involved with the university and provides assistance with the broadcasting of Tennessee Football games.

Coach Wyant is my hero for many reasons. I have applied the lessons I learned from my time playing for him throughout my life. He has an exceptional track record of success and accomplishments in college athletics and in business. He has always been organized and paid attention to details. He had determination and was always a leader and problem-solver. He was a great mentor and motivator. Most importantly, Coach was a great husband, father, and friend. He was dependable and never let you down. He married his high school sweetheart, Betty, and they were together for over 50 years. His care for Betty following her debilitating stroke in 1994 is truly a testament to his loyalty, dedication, commitment, and love of his wife and family. Betty passed away in 2011. Coach Wyant and Betty have three children: Greg, Mike, and Jennifer. All three are college graduates and are successful in their careers. The Wyant family includes nine grandchildren and two great-grandchildren. The family continues to move forward because of their positive leader — Coach!

Coach Wyant's son, Greg, followed in his father's footsteps and became a coach and athletic director at the high school level. Greg remembers special times, lasting memories, and lessons learned with his father. He shared his fond memories of going to many bowl games and having the opportunities to go on the practice fields and into the locker room following games.

Coach Gary Wyant has made a positive difference in the lives of so many, and he has made things better wherever he walked and worked. He is special to so many! A son of the "greatest generation," he always got it done; he always made a Case for the Defense! And, if you couldn't tell, I love the guy!

LESSONS LEARNED FROM COACH WYANT

Coach taught us to not stand around the pile, but to get on it. He would say, "Put your bonnet on it." If you are standing around the pile somebody is going to "clean your clock," and that is how you will get injured. He also taught us to always go "full speed" and then you have the momentum and advantage when you make contact with the opponent.

I have carried that advice into my life and career, and it served me well. I learned to not stand around, but to get involved and get into the action. Also, if you approach your career with vigor and determination going "full speed," you will have momentum when you meet the competition and you will seize the opportunity.

Good advice and it made a difference for me and other members of the "Rat Pack."

Coach Bob Harbison - FSU Legend Defensive Coach 1948-1986

CHAPTER 17

BOB HARBISON

This timeless story about legendary FSU Coach Bob Harbison was originally prepared in September 2006 by FSU sports historian Judge James (Jim) Joanos for the Seminole Boosters. It appeared in the "Report to Boosters." The article was titled "Garnet and Old, A look Back at a Legend, Harbie." With Judge Joanos' approval, it is reprinted below with a few minor additions and modification of length.

COACH'S COMMENT   "A thoughtful listener and when he spoke, everybody listened." — Coach Bowden

Florida State has been blessed with lots of outstanding assistant football coaches during the years. There is one that many of us refer to as "The Legend." His 37 seasons on the staff for seven different head coaches is longer than any other football coach has ever served on the FSU staff.

Bob Harbison came to FSU in 1948, one year after the school took up football in the modern era, with newly hired head coach Don Veller. He coached at FSU every year thereafter through the 1986 season with the exception of the 1973 season when he sat out a season. Shortly after Harbison retired, the famed and beloved Tallahassee Democrat sports writer, Bill McGrotha, pointed out that the "story of Harbie has, at times, approached the legendary among many Seminoles. Some think he hung the moon."

"Harbie," as he is popularly known, unquestionably has been one of the most important people in the development of FSU football. In 1947, FSU selected Don Veller to become its head coach. Harbie was one of three assistants whom Veller hired to round out his coaching staff. The other two were brothers, Charlie and Bill Armstrong. The Armstrongs had also played their college football at Indiana. The coaching responsibilities were divided with Harbison and Charlie Armstrong coaching the linemen while Veller and Bill Armstrong coached the backs. At the time players customarily played both offense and defense as the rules limited substitution.

Harbison grew up on a farm in Petersburg, Indiana. One of his school classmates, a brother of baseball great Gil Hodges, talked Harbison into going out for football. The school was so small that it played six-man football. In his junior year he moved on to Evanston, Indiana and finished high school there where he first played the standard 11-man football. Playing football turned out to be a good decision as Harbison went on to the University of Indiana where he not only played college football on a championship team, he continued his education. When Veller asked Harbison to join him in Tallahassee, Harbie welcomed the opportunity as it seemed a great deal more interesting to him than his other alternatives of getting a job in a coal mine or going back to Petersburg and a career in farming.

Harbison is known for a number of special attributes. They include his success as a recruiter, his ability to scout an opposing team and his skill in coaching linemen. Gene McDowell, the former head coach at the University of Central Florida, said that Harbison, "is, if not the best, one of the best recruiters he has ever known." McDowell knows Harbie as one of his coaches when he played at

FSU, as well as a fellow assistant coach, and as a personal friend. McDowell served as an assistant at FSU along with Harbie for a number of seasons. McDowell explains that the characteristic that made Harbison a premier recruiter was "his ability to recognize talent." He said that Harbison could watch a high school player perform and determine whether or not he could play at Florida State.

There are numerous stories about players whom Harbison recruited for FSU. Some of those stories include the recruitment of Deion Sanders. They have to do with the low key and soft spoken, no-bull Harbison, and his reaction to the flamboyant Sanders. They tell of how Sanders, a high school option quarterback, who was being recruited by very few other schools to play football, was spotted by Harbison. Harbie saw that Sanders had the attributes that would make him an excellent college football player for FSU. An interesting relationship developed between them. The end result was Sanders resisted a high-powered recruitment process by the Kansas City Royals, who desperately wanted Sanders to sign with them to play baseball. The process included almost daily telephone calls from the Royals. Ultimately, as you know, Harbison's recruit became one of the very best athletes ever to play for the Seminoles.

There are stories about the success that Harbison had in recruiting players out of Leon High School when he had the local Tallahassee area as his recruiting assignment. The stories describe the "Leon Connection" and the relationship between Harbison and the local high school in the mid '70s when Gene Cox, a FSU football alumnus was the coach at Leon and producing powerhouse championship teams. For several years there were five or more players from that same high school that were part of the FSU teams that under "new coach" Bobby Bowden were building the foundation for the Seminoles' move into the upper echelons of American college football.

Three of the players on FSU's team during Coach Bowden's second season when the team went 10-2 were Leon players that Harbison helped recruit: quarterbacks Wally Woodam and Jimmy Jordan, and defensive back Ivory Joe Hunter. That was FSU's first ever 10-win team. FSU finished the year in 14th place in the AP national rankings, the highest finish that FSU had ever attained up to that time. Harbison also used old ties to recruit for FSU. To pick up Lane Fenner, Harbie spotted him at Harbie's own former high school in Evansville, Indiana, and persuaded the lanky receiver to come to FSU. At FSU, Fenner received a great deal of notoriety when he made the famous would-be winning touchdown catch thrown by Gary Pajcic, another Harbison recruit, against Florida in 1966 that was ruled out of bounds. Seminole fans simply refer to that play as "The Catch."

There is also a wonderful story about how Harbie tried to recruit another player from the State of Indiana. Harbie even got the kid to come to Florida State on a recruiting visit. Unfortunately, the other coaches on the team nixed Harbison's recruit as being unfit for college football as the prospect was "too fat and did not look like a college player." As a result, Alex Karras ended up at the University of Iowa where he won the Outland Trophy after his senior season as the nation's best lineman of the year. Karras later starred in the NFL for many years, was a professional wrestler, and movie actor and has been inducted into college football's Hall of Fame. When reminded of Karras, Harbison smiles. He is quick to say that he, "did miss some good ones, too." He chuckles and mentions Jack Youngblood from nearby Monticello in whom Harbie "did not see a lot." Youngblood, thereafter, walked on at the University of Florida and became a most outstanding player and later starred in the NFL. As a further illustration, he points out that in recruiting quarterback Gary Pajcic, who was very much in demand, he learned that Pajcic had a very close friend and that the two desired to go to the same college. Although the close friend was "too skinny for football" Harbison got FSU to offer both. That is why Ron Sellers, an all time great receiver, was recruited and came to FSU. Harbie concludes, "you have to be lucky too." Harbie to this day says that "recruiting is the game in this league." "You cannot win the Kentucky Derby with a donkey."

Scouting opposing teams — Being informed of other teams, their abilities, techniques and tendencies has always been important in football. During most of the years that Harbie coached, the methods for doing that were very different from the present ways. Then you did not have much in the way of previous game films, nor the computerized technology and staff assistants now available with which to break down and understand the propensities of the opposing teams. Instead, it was customary to have each of the individual assistant coaches in addition to their other responsibilities, held responsible for the gathering of information about opposing teams. When the week of the game against that team came, a previously designated assistant coach would brief the rest of the coaches. They also had a major role in developing the game plan for that specific game. Harbie describes it thusly: "Everybody had a team or two. You would have one or two teams. You would collect, cut out newspaper clippings, and post them on the bulletin board. It made you feel special about that game." Head coach Bill Peterson is reported to saying Harbie was called "Eagle Eye." Jim Selman, a sports writer for the Tampa Tribune, wrote in a 1978 article that Harbison earned that nickname because of the precise scouting reports he turned in on opposing teams. Also, in that article, he quotes Peterson as saying, "what he presented, the kids respected." Selman also quoted longtime and very knowledgeable FSU Trainer, Don Fauls as saying that "75 to 80 percent of the games he scouted for us, we won." Winning 75 to 80 percent of our games during most of those years was astronomical.

Coaching Skills — When you talk to former players who were coached by Harbison, one of the things that they remember most was he was a very competent teacher. Harbison has, throughout his coaching career, been a line coach. In 1948, when he came to FSU and for a number of years thereafter, players played both ways, on offense and defense. Consequently, he had to coach linemen to play on both sides of the ball. After the rules changed and free substitution was allowed in the '60s, Harbie coached defensive linemen. He also became the team's Defensive Coordinator. In his first season in that capacity, Harbie organized FSU's first great defensive team, which became known widely as featuring the "Seven Magnificents," and the "Forgotten Four." Just prior to the 1964's season beginning, each of the seven linemen and linebackers had their heads shaved in Yul Brynner fashion. At the time, a movie Brynner starred in, "The Magificent Seven," had just become established as a classic film. Similarly, Harbison's "Seven Magnificents Defensive team" has become "a classic" in FSU football history. Nearly every book written about the overall history of FSU football includes photos of that team and those shaved heads. The defensive team began the 1964 season by holding all three of the teams FSU played scoreless during that 9-1-1 season, which culminated in a win over Oklahoma in the Gator Bowl. All of FSU's opponents together only scored 85 points, compared to the Seminoles' 263. This was fewer than 8 points per game.

Harbie was exceptionally talented at developing defensive schemes. It seemed he had a good scheme for every team FSU faced. Whether it was a running team or a pass crazy one, he seemed to have an answer. When asked about his ability to defend against various offenses, he responded by saying that "you have to have a package ... a variety. When you run into a hot receiver, maybe you can double on him, and your team is familiar with doing that. You need a whole system."

Of all the defensive plays called during his coaching, he is proudest of one special call which he terms "the best call I ever made." It was in the Gator Bowl game following the 1967 regular season. Penn State, under the second-year coach Joe Paterno, was dominating the Seminoles. It was early in the third quarter and the Nitanny Lions were leading FSU 17-0. Harbie admits that up to that point, he had been "fooled a time or two" by Paterno's offense. Then with the ball on Penn State's own 15 yard-line and fourth and inches to go, Paterno, still very confident in his offense, decided to go for it. At first Harbie had his punt return team ready to go in, but when he saw that Penn State's punter was not entering the field of play, he immediately changed his strategy. However, instead of putting in a safe and more conservative defensive alignment, he took a big risk and put in the "goal line defense." According to a few defensive players from that era, Penn State failed to get the required inches on an attempted quarterback sneak due to an alleged poor spot by the referees. FSU defensive back Johnny Crowe, reported that in the pile-up at the point of attack, Mike Blatt actually pushed the quarterback back about a half yard from his forward momentum position. Due to the crowd of bodies around the football, Penn State could not regain the half yard they presumably lost in the melee. FSU took over the ball and the game. Immediately thereafter, FSU's famed passing tandem of Kim Hammond to Ron Sellers completed a quick touchdown pass. The Seminoles later scored another touchdown and in closing moments kicked a field goal to end the game in a 17 to 17 tie. Harbison enjoys reminiscing about that game. He adds a footnote that, a few years later, on a visit to Penn State when he had an opportunity to be in Coach Paterno's office, he noticed a sign prominently displayed, that said simply, "When in doubt, punt." It is one of Harbie's fondest memories of a lifetime in coaching.

When Bill Peterson left FSU after the 1970 season, Larry Jones became the head coach. Jones' experience was primarily as a defensive coach, so the head coach took over the over-all responsibility for the defense. Harbison was moved over to the other side of the ball and became the offensive line coach where he would coach thereafter. Harbison did not mind as he says "he was getting old" and coaching offense was "less physical" than defense. He adds, "In coaching defense you have to get out there with the players and mix it up with them. Offense does not require the same kind of physical stuff." He had coached offensive techniques in his early years at FSU, so did not find it difficult to adjust. He proved to be an excellent offensive line coach and continued in that capacity under head coach Darrel Mudra, and into the first 10 of the Bobby Bowden years.

Harbison trained his linemen very hard but was very fortunate to suffer limited injuries. One interesting technique that he employed was to have his linemen do their practice hitting less than a yard apart. In that way, "you could hit for a long time and not get hurt much." One player that he regards as an outstanding offensive lineman was Ken Lanier who played for FSU from 1977 to 1980. After college, Lanier played in the NFL, mostly for the Denver Broncos. Harbie says that "Lanier could do everything you asked of him." When asked about his coaching skills, he describes it "like anything else." "It is having people listen to what you are trying to teach them. If they believe in what you are telling them, you can get them to believe they will win. If not, you have trouble. The more success you have the more you believe."

Retirement: Harbison retired in 1986. Shortly thereafter he was inducted into the FSU Athletic Hall of Fame. In looking back over his career, he says, "it has been an interesting life. I have griped a lot but I have never wanted to do anything else." In retirement, Harbison has been able to do a lot of things that he did not have "time to do earlier." He fishes and hunts often as he loves the outdoors. He also reads a lot, saying that in reading, he discovers some "strange things." Currently, he is reading a book about Ernest Hemingway that includes stories the famous writer wrote in his early years as a newspaper reporter in Toronto. Bob and wife Jane were able to take time for nice vacations. For 15 straight summers they enjoyed extended fishing vacations with former FSU player and popular actor, Bob Urich. That pattern ended only upon Urich's death a few years ago. The Harbisons would visit Urich and his family at their cottage in Canada and stay in their guest house. Harbie admits, "How strange it was the first time, to be holding a light in a boat at night for a famous movie star that was wading in the water trying to catch night crawlers." Harbison's wife, Jane, died suddenly this past summer. They had been married for 58 years. It hit him very hard, but he is "handling it" well. Fortunately, he has close contact with their children and lots of friends who have helped make it bearable. He continues to involve himself in interesting activities and is positive about the future.

Lots of Harbie's former players and coaching colleagues stay in touch with him on a regular basis. When asked to name some of his favorites, he would not. There are "too many of them and I might leave someone out," was his reply. Although Bob Harbison uses words very sparingly, he is a master in communicating. He can say more in a few words than most people can in a paragraph. His short, succinct answers to inquiries are remarkable. In 1970, Tampa Tribune writer, recognized this trait of Harbie and wrote, "Harbie speaks quietly and seldom, but when he makes an utterance, it usually means something." It is easy to see why Harbie is a great coach, a great teacher of men. He captivates people with his candid statements and ability to go immediately to the key point. If you listen to him carefully, you can learn a lot very quickly about the inner workings of football, but more importantly about what is most important in life. "Wise" is the best word I can come up with in describing Harbison, who has been a family friend since he came to Tallahassee. Florida State is very fortunate that Bob Harbison has been here to help develop the football program into one of the best.

COACH'S COMMENT "Best all-around coach I have worked with. Good listener and creative with hybrid defense schemes." — Coach Wyant

COACHES PLAYBOOK

Johnny Crowe

Judge Jim Joanos shared a playbook that Coach Harbison gave him during an interview many years ago. It truly was a treasure for the 1960 football season. I spent several hours reviewing the very inclusive playbook and the summaries of the games that year. It was a fantastic experience. I pulled several comments and statements from the playbook that support our Case for the Defense.

1. No team has ever gained a national reputation without being tough defensively. Your defense will be based on TOUGHNESS, HUSTLE, and UNITY! Individual mistakes will hurt the over-all defensive picture, but SECOND EFFORT by everyone will make up for that individual mistake.

2. Our defenses are disguised so one looks like the other. Only on the snap of the ball and your charge will change the strength of the defense. Expect the team to gain on you, but be ready to take the ball away by fumble, interception, or blocked punt. Make them go the hard way. Team speed and second effort will do this — give them more opportunities to make a mistake.

3. Our toughest defense is always played inside our own 10-yard line.

4. WE WILL WIN OR LOSE ON PASS DEFENSE! Rush the passer — most important phase! Must have effort to get the passer down or force him to throw in a hurry which will increase pass interceptions. A good rush will keep a receiver from going long. Cover the receiver — second most important phase! We will always cover deep receivers. The long completed pass will defeat you. Break down the timing of receivers — In all defenses, someone is in front of the offensive end so he cannot get out freely. You must make him pay a price to get out.

5. Pass defense is a team effort.[4] When a long pass is completed on us for a touchdown, in most cases it is because of a loafing lineman. We expect a team to complete short passes. Short gains with runs or passes will not defeat you.

6. Team Unity — encourage, don't discourage. Understand your responsibility as well as your teammate's responsibility. Gang tackle. We must eliminate our opponents' backs from falling forward. Always keep in mind that every play could be the one that wins or loses the ball game for you, so play defense accordingly. Remember defense is team play. Hang tough together.

7. IF A TEAM CAN'T SCORE ON US, THEY CAN'T BEAT US.

8. THE ONLY TIME THERE IS NO OFFENSIVE TEAM OR DEFENSIVE TEAM IS WHEN THE BALL IS IN THE AIR. IT BELONGS TO THE TEAM THAT GOES AFTER IT.

---

4. Wow, as a defensive back, I love this next sentence. It forgives me for every bad coverage in my career!

Seminole Head Coach Bill Peterson 1960–1970, record 62-42-11

CHAPTER 18

TRIBUTE TO COACH BILL PETERSON

Dale McCullers

C oach Peterson was much more than a brilliant gridiron strategist. He was more than an offensive innovator and a popular Seminole football coach.

Despite all the hoopla about his comical verbal expressions — he had a habit of scrambling or inverting words and their meanings — he was also a competent and resourceful leader. He was always organized and busy, but easily entreated. He was tall and strong. He was well-dressed and neat in appearance. He carried himself like a proud peacock. His countenance was usually animated and pleasant for the most part, unless he was coaching, worried, or upset about something that is; then you had better listen or face a stern lecture. He was strong-willed and could express his feelings when making a point. In brief, he was definitely in command, and he was determined to have things done his way.

The odd syntax or mixed up metaphors — the so-called "Petersonisms" — somehow always made perfect sense to me as a young man, which should tell you something about my own quirks and idiosyncrasies. Although some of Coach Pete's odd statements may have been jumbled up, they somehow filled the psychological space in my head with positive thoughts. One of my favorites was, "You guys line up alphabetically by height."

On a personal note, he erroneously kept calling me "Jack" in team meetings. I figured out he was confusing me with Jack Shinholser, a middle guard who played for the Seminoles during the 1963 to 1966 era. As chronicled in Chapter 8, Jack was a famed member of the "Seven Magnificents" defensive line. Since Jack is now an FSU Athletic Hall of Fame inductee, I consider it an honor to be called "Jack," even if my name is Dale. A lot of my teammates called me "Jack McCullers," poking fun at Coach Pete and loudly calling me by my new name in the locker room. Despite all the zaniness about jumbling words and reinventing the Queen's English, Coach Pete's demeanor and expressions instilled in me a desire to perform better. As comical as they were, his statements somehow fostered quiet reflection and firm resolve to do your best in games. Players trusted Coach Pete's counsel, as odd as it was at times.

We all knew that Coach Pete was intelligent. He knew the game of football. He understood what it took in terms of sacrifice to win football games. I can't explain it, but his zany "Petersonisms" somehow gave his players an opportunity to do a mental exercise, which often helped us gain a psychological edge in games. I think it was sometimes so odd that it made you really ponder hard and look for the symbolism or hidden meaning in his commentary. A good example was once before a game, he said: "just remember the words of Henry Patrick: kill me or let me live!" I thought on that one real hard. In my mind's eye came an image of me fighting to the death on the football field against a fierce opponent. The symbolism was clear as glass, in a foggy kind of way. I can truthfully say I admired and loved Coach Pete, even though as a young man, I was sometimes a knuckle-head and didn't give Coach Pete the respect he deserved. In 1993, news of his death at the relatively young age of 73 deeply saddened me. It was like losing a favorite big brother. I am not ashamed to say that I teared up. I also reflected deeply on the positive impact his teachings made in my life.

I feel compelled to share, now in my 70th year of age, one personal story of when I angered Coach Pete; I also likely disappointed him. This unfortunate incident happened due to my youthful and naive, unwise, and unruly tongue during one of Coach Pete's fiery halftime speeches. He gave this particular halftime lecture when we were getting beat by North Carolina State over 50 years ago in 1967.

At half time, Coach Pete essentially pitched a tantrum about our poor performance versus North Carolina State. He told us with great contempt and animation that we were "running scared" and playing like we were intimidated or afraid. He didn't say we were girly men or sissies, but my male pride and ego took it that way. He seemed to be highly agitated, bordering on a complete meltdown but still under control. All of my teammates, except for me, had the good sense to take his tongue-lashing and keep quiet. However, even though I had a reputation for being usually quiet and reserved, (except if I was agitated myself), I blurted out, "You need to shut up, we're not afraid!"

Everyone but "good ole Jack McCullers" discerned that his fiery speech was purposely designed to make us fighting mad, to make us play better. Coach Pete immediately pointed his finger at me and said, "McCullers, you haven't played worth a flip today. You need to watch yourself!" I was stunned. I felt sick and dumb as a stick at the same time. I felt kind of like an empty uniform with nobody inside it, looking for a place to hide. I meant what I said, although I was embarrassed at my lack of self-control. The following Monday afternoon I was summoned to Coach Pete's office before practice.

I was in full pads, sitting and waiting in his office with my helmet in my hand in case I needed to put it on quickly. He walked in the room like a proverbial peacock, sat down at his desk, and suddenly smiled at me. He then essentially told me from now on to leave the half-time speeches to him alone. Once he had chewed me out and shared how low I was on the ladder, he shook my hand in an act of acceptance and good will.

To this day, I am unfortunately reminded of my disrespectful slip of the tongue by former teammates at reunions.

After graduating in 1969, because I was undersized at a little over six feet, and weighing 198 pounds, my chances to play pro football seemed slim. Unbeknownst to me, during the 1969 professional draft, Coach Pete personally called the Miami Dolphins and convinced them to draft me in the 12th round, sparking my professional football career.

I have never forgotten the noble traits and innate goodness of Coach Pete. Shortly after being chewed out by him in his office, I was invited to travel with him and a few other players, all of us riding in his big Cadillac, to my hometown as guest speakers at our 1968 high school sports banquet. We engaged in small talk on the trip, and I told him I was a little nervous about speaking before a group. Later that night he made me relax, and I got a good laugh when he told me on the dais, "Don't be nervous, everyone in the audience puts on their underpants one arm and leg at a time, just like us." Go figure.

COMMENTS ON COACH PETE
John Crowe

Coach Pete was a dedicated professional and innovator, a pioneer in bringing pro-style offense to college football. He had a great teacher in Sid Gillman of the San Diego Chargers. Coach Pete spent time with Coach Gillman to perfect the offensive style he brought to FSU. Pete is remembered for several significant accomplishments, including the first ever home and away victories over the Gators; the first major bowl victory in the Gator Bowl with a convincing win over renowned program at Oklahoma; ties with Alabama and Penn State; and for giving FSU the opportunity to recruit with the big time programs in Florida and the nation.

Fair or not, most often, mine and others' memories are some of his malaprops that became known as "Petersonisms." Everyone has favorites, and I am no different. It is easy to recall his many statements and expressions, and it is difficult to stop once you get started telling them. Coach Pete, like Yogi Berra, claimed he got credit for many quotes that weren't his, but Coach Pete told me that was OK with him, as he liked the attention, and it added to the legend.

I believe that his ability to put words and phrases together in such a unique and careless way was clearly creative and even borderline genius. Many true keepers of the art of speaking would certainly disagree, but I would argue that the point Coach Pete was trying to capture would be remembered longer, given the way he mixed up words and their relations to a particular subject. For example, when he told us, "Men, pair off in threes and line up in a circle, alphabetical by height." What I believe he meant was for us to stick together and cover each other's back in an organized and innovative way. Maybe this is a stretch, but that's my story, and I am sticking with it.

I remember so many things that Coach Pete taught us, and the learnings are still with me today.

I particularly remember a lesson about teamwork and the importance of being a team player. There is seldom anything significant that was accomplished by one person; it takes teamwork, with each person playing his position or role with excellence and in harmony with others. Second, if you surround yourself with dedicated and talented people and then work to make them successful, they will take you to a level of achievement that is far greater than you could have imagined.

Those lessons served me well as a defensive back, an Air Force pilot, and as a CEO with Buckeye Technologies. In my journey through life, being part of a team was the central theme.

Looking back at "The Peterson years," the list of coaches that Coach Pete brought to Florida State is very impressive and was a key reason for the success we had in the 1960s that set the stage for things to come. At the high risk that I will miss some deserving coaches, I want to provide the coaches that Coach Pete had on his staff to demonstrate my thesis. Here is a list of coaches that developed the Sons of the Sixties: Vince Gibson, Don James, Don Powell, Bob Harbison, Ken Meyer, Bobby Bowden, Bobby Jackson, Gary Wyant, Joe Gibbs, Don Breaux, Al Conover, Gene McDowell, Dan Henning, Bill Parcells, and Bud Whitehead.

You may or may not have realized the quality of coaches that Coach Pete had on his staff, but you will have to agree the list is impressive and it reads like a "Who's Who" of college coaches. These coaches have stories of their years at FSU and all of whom I have spoken with have praised Coach Pete for the learnings they had developing their personal skills and style while at FSU. And yes, they all have funny stories about Coach Pete that make him a special person in their lives.

Coach Pete loved FSU and college football. I believe that is why Coach Pete, like so many former coaches, returned to Tallahassee when they retired. Coach Pete would have preferred to have never left Tallahassee when he moved on to Rice University and later as head coach of the Houston Oilers.

Dale and I owe Coach Pete for providing us the opportunity to play football and get our degrees at FSU. He is gone, but not forgotten: Pete's poles still stand on Bobby Bowden field.

FSU one time! FSU all the damn time!

Now that Johnny and I have shared some of our personal insights, reflections, and memories about Coach Pete from a Seminole football player's perspective, you're probably interested in learning about Coach Bill Peterson. If you wish to read a great biographical summary about former FSU Head Coach Peterson, check out an article prepared by legendary FSU sports historian Judge Jim Joanos. This article was originally written in 2010 for the Wakulla Times Newspaper, entitled "Seminole Spotlight — Remembering Bill Peterson." The entire article can be found on the website NoleFan.org.

CHAPTER 19
LEGENDARY FSU DEFENSIVE COACHES

John Crowe

Coaches Bowden, Gladden, and Andrews were willing to sit with me in separate interviews and provide me with their philosophy about defensive football that supports our efforts to make A Case for the Defense. Each of them had a legendary career and are members of the FSU Athletic Hall of Fame.

FSU Head Coach Bobby Bowden - 1976 - 2009

BOBBY BOWDEN — A CASE FOR THE DEFENSE

I had the honor and great opportunity to sit with an American legend to discuss college football with a focus on the defensive team and strategy. Coach Bowden doesn't need my introduction to explain what he has accomplished and meant to college football. If you haven't seen the film "The Bowden Dynasty," you should. If you have, then you know what I mean.

Always ready to serve, Coach Bobby Bowden was interested in helping Dale and me with "FSU's Sons of the Sixties — A Case for the Defense." I recently had the opportunity to attend FSU spring practice on the same day Coach Bowden came to speak with the Seminole players at the invitation of new head coach, Willie Taggart. I briefly explained the theme of our book and asked if I could get his thoughts about it. Coach didn't hesitate and said, "Call me if I can help you in anyway."

On May 22, I sat down with Coach Bowden and explained what we wanted to capture about the sons of the Greatest Generation that came to FSU in the sixties and who used the football scholarships they were awarded to fulfill their parents' dream of seeing their sons graduate from college. He understood the theme and lived it, growing up in a middle-income family using his athletic skills to earn an athletic scholarship first to the University of Alabama and then to Howard College (later Samford) to play college football, baseball, and track.

I enjoyed spending time with Coach Bowden, listening to his thoughts on the importance of having a strong, capable defensive unit. Coach said, "I was raised on defense and as a head coach, I made it the #1 priority." During the first meeting with his staff after becoming the head coach at FSU in 1975, he said, "I want to put the fastest and toughest kids on defense. If our opponents can't score, they can't win. Then I want an offense that doesn't hurt our defense." There you have it, from the legendary coach, a strong endorsement and a "Case for the Defense!"

I first met Coach Bowden when I was a freshman in 1965. Coach Bowden had an impact on me then, and he did again on the day of our interview.

He was interested in our book's theme and was so gracious, humble, and alert. His memory of players and situations was fantastic. He had no problem recalling names of players, coaches, and game results. He remembered the 1964 season, and the first time an FSU team was ranked in the AP Top Ten, something he would later repeat for 14 consecutive seasons — the Dynasty Years from 1987 to 2000! He praised the 1964 team and coaches for the great success they had and said, "I learned from Coach Peterson the importance of a solid coaching staff in the years I was an FSU assistant. If you surround yourself with very competent coaches, you will produce winning teams." It is interesting to note that Coach Bowden seldom uses the pronoun "I" but talks about his staff and the team and gives them the credit for the many victories and records.

Coach has made a positive impact on so many. He is a man of faith and doesn't hide it. I heard Derrick Brooks speak at a Fellowship of Christian Athletes annual event last year, and he told the audience how Coach Bowden would sit with some of the players the night before the games and share his faith. One evening, Coach Bowden posed the question, "If you died tonight, would you go to heaven or hell?" Derrick said, "As I was thinking about the question, Coach said, 'if you have to think about it, you are probably going to hell.'" Derrick said, "That made an impression on me and how I lived my life. Now, I no longer have to think about it!" What a great question!

The number of books, articles, and reports on Coach Bobby Bowden are numerous, and he is probably still the best-known college football coach in America — and even beyond our borders. On a visit to London several years ago, I noticed as I passed the display window at Harrods department store a mannequin dressed to look like Coach Bobby Bowden. Even in England they know Bobby Bowden!

The time I spent sitting and discussing defensive football with Coach Bowden will be a day I will never forget! As I was leaving on that day, Coach Bowden talked about how he had been blessed. I believe so many of us have been blessed to know Coach Bobby Bowden. Coach has had some great moments, but he has also had difficult times in his life recovering from rheumatic fever as a youth and losing two grandsons and a son-in-law to automobile accidents. His faith has seen him through those troubled times and still guides his life.

Coach Bowden was inducted into the FSU Athletic Hall of Fame in 2012. The following was the citation for his selection:

Florida State Head Football Coach for 34 years from 1976 to 2009 and the Wide Receivers Coach from 1963 to '65 ... his record at Florida State was 316-97-4 including a record of 85-60-1 against ranked teams ... took his team to 31 bowl games and compiled a 22-8-1 record ... Florida State has enjoyed a trip to a bowl game his last 28 years, since 1982 ... had a bowl record of 13-0-1 from 1982 through 1995 ... won two national championships in 1993 and wire-to-wire #1 in 1999 ... coached 153 All-Americans including 25 NCAA Consensus All-Americans ... coached award winners: Paul McGowan (Butkus), Deion Sanders (Thorpe), Terrell Buckley (Thorpe), Casey Weldon (Unitas), Marvin Jones (Lombardi, Butkus), Charlie Ward (Heisman, Maxwell, Camp, O'Brien, Unitas), Sebastian Janikowski (Groza-twice), Chris Weinke (Heisman, O'Brien, Unitas), Jamal Reynolds (Lombardi), and Graham Gano (Groza) ... one of his players, Myron Rolle, earned a Rhodes Scholarship ... 177 of his players were drafted by NFL teams, 32 in the first round, and because of free agents, 197 played in the NFL ... from 1987 through 2000 FSU won at least 10 games a year and finished in the top five in the polls ... the NCAA designated Florida State as a Dynasty from 1987 to 2000 ... second winningest coach in major college football history ... Bowden was named National Coach of the Year six times and in 2004 the National Citizenship Award from the Fellowship of Christian Athletes was named after him ... he was inducted into the College Football Hall of Fame in 2006 ... words to describe him include respect, sincerity, class, honesty, charisma, charm, and humor ... he is a man of faith, strength and integrity.

I came away from my interview with Coach Bowden with a few key learn-ings. Coach Bowden believes in role models, and his was the famed Coach General Bob Neyland at the University of Tennessee. Most of Coach Bowden's early experiences were affiliated with the University of Tennessee and Coach Neyland. Coach Bowden is a great role model!

Coach Bowden played offense and defense and was always involved in coaching both offense and defense. The experience made him aware of the value of having a dominating defense. Coach said, "If the opponent can't score, they can't beat you!" It may sound simple, but it works!

As a head coach, he was involved setting direction and expectations for both the offense and the defense coaches. He would set the expectations and then let them do their jobs. He said, "If I had to interfere, I didn't need that coach." He believes that you put the fastest and toughest play-ers on defense, and to prove his point he gave me several examples: Ron Simmons, Marvin Jones, Paul McGowan, Deion Sanders, Derrick Brooks, Bobby Butler, and Terrell Buckley, to name a few great Seminole defensive stars. He summarized good defensive players as those who are quick, able to run, love the contact, and have a feel for the game.

JIM GLADDEN AND MICKEY ANDREWS — CASES FOR THE DEFENSE

A book about Florida State football with a focus on the defense would be incomplete without comments from two of the greatest defensive coaches in college football history, Jim Gladden and Mickey Andrews. I was fortunate to be able to sit down with these two significant contributors to the "Bowden Dynasty."

FSU Defensive Coach Jim Gladden - 1975-2001

Jim Gladden was part of the FSU football staff from 1975 to 2001, coaching linebackers and defensive ends. He also had a significant role in specialty teams, particularly punt and kick blocking. FSU had great success blocking kicks for over two decades. He coached many All-Americans and had a record number of first round draft choices. Coach Gladden still has great relationships with many former athletes!

Coach Gladden was inducted into the FSU Athletic Hall of Fame in 2018 and the following is the citation for his selection:

> For 27 years (1975 to 2001), Jim Gladden coached football at Florida State where he was on coaching staffs that elevated Florida State's program into the most consistently successful in college football history.
>
> Gladden joined then-head coach Darrell Mudra's coaching staff in 1975 as a graduate assistant and was elevated to a full-time position in 1976, when the legendary Bobby Bowden took over the program. He coached outside linebackers for Bowden from 1976 through 1995 and switched to defensive ends coach from 1996 until his retirement in 2001.
>
> Gladden coached and recruited some of the greatest names in Seminole history including NFL Hall of Famer Derrick Brooks, and

FSU Hall of Famers Peter Boulware, Reinard Wilson, Andre Wadsworth, and Jamal Reynolds.

A personable and highly successful recruiter, Gladden was also highly regarded for his ability to judge talent. Additionally, he coached FSU's legendary punt block unit that blocked 80 over his tenure.

The Seminoles won National Championships in 1993 and 1999 during Gladden's tenure and played for titles three more times. While the fact that FSU earned a bowl berth in each of the last 23 years of his career is stunning, even more impressive is Florida State's record 14 straight Top 5 finishes from 1987 to 2000, which has never been matched in the history of the game.

FSU Defensive Coach Mickey Andrews - 1984 - 2009

Mickey Andrews, an All-American wide receiver and cornerback at Alabama in 1964, came to FSU in 1984 after many successful years of coaching, including winning the NAIA Division 1 National Championship as head coach of Livingston University (known today as University of West Alabama) in 1971. Coach Andrews coached defensive backs at FSU for 26 seasons before retiring in 2009. He had numerous All-American defensive backs, including two Jim Thorpe award winners, Deion Sanders and Terrell Buckley. As defensive coordinator, Coach Andrews consistently had nationally ranked defensive units, and his 1998 defensive unit was ranked #1 nationally in total defense and pass defense.

In 2010, Coach Andrews was inducted into the FSU Athletic Hall of Fame with the following citation for his selection:

> Mickey Andrews came to Florida State in 1984 as the defensive coordinator and immediately began to build a defense that matched the Seminoles' high-powered offense, creating a dynasty the likes of which college football had never seen. He would coach at FSU for 26 years before retiring after the 2009 season.
>
> An All-SEC defensive back at Alabama (1961-64), Andrews won a national championship as head coach at North Alabama in 1976. He went on to serve as an assistant coach at Clemson, Florida, and for the USFL's Arizona Wranglers before Bobby Bowden chose him as his right-hand man and the FSU program vaulted to the hierarchy of college football. FSU would finish among the Associated Press Top 5 for an unprecedented 14 straight seasons and won its two national titles, 1993 and 1999, during Andrews' tenure.
>
> Andrews' defenses developed into feared units that combined blazing speed and relentless pressure. He coached many of the biggest names in college football history including 19 first-round NFL draft picks, 74 drafted players and, because of free agency, 82 athletes who have played in the NFL.
>
> He was named the nation's top assistant coach in 2000 by the All-American Football Foundation and 1991 by Athlon's Magazine. He was named the national defensive coordinator of the year in 1998 by American Football Coaches' Magazine and was the first-ever winner of the Frank Broyles Award as nation's top assistant in 1996.

Andrews coached 51 All-Americans and 13 NCAA Consensus All-Americans, two Jim Thorpe Award winners, two Butkus Award winners, and two Lombardi Award winners.

Coach Gladden and Coach Andrews both understood the value of a strong defensive unit and how it can make the difference for a winning program. Both are Sons of the Sixties, growing up during difficult times and developing strong work ethics and family values from parents of the Greatest Generation. Life was tough, and that's just the way it was in the 1940s and 1950s. Like Coach Bowden, Coach Gladden and Coach Andrews were raised to work hard and to be in church when the doors were open. Their strong faith is key to how they coached and lived their lives. These men are great role models and they make a great "Case for the Defense!"

I tried to capture their key comments in what follows.

Coach Gladden – May 25, 2018

Coach Gladden shared the defensive principles he learned from 40 years of coaching and what he calls "trial and error." These principles served FSU well during the Bowden Dynasty years.

Coach said,

> First, dependability is more important than ability, however, skills are important. You want to put the players with speed and quickness on defense, and if you don't have it, you end up chasing it. Coach Gladden wanted young men who were collusion experts with intelligent intensity and wanted to see 11 helmets after the ball carrier on every snap. Players will do what the coaches demand of them and if you can keep it simple it will be easier to execute. While two top ingredients for a successful defensive unit are hitters and runners, morale is the single most important factor. If morale is high, the kids will have fun and be of one heartbeat! While offense is assignment football, defense is reaction football. To play

defense you must be able to separate from the blockers, run to the ball and then make the tackle. If you can't, you better play offense.

Coach Gladden had five rules in recruiting:

1. Can he graduate from FSU?

2. Can he run?

3. Is he dependable?

4. Will he fight and not quit?

5. Can we beat the Gators with him?

Coach Mickey Andrews – May 26th, 2018

Coach Andrews grew up playing sports and particularly liked the defensive side of the field in football. His experiences and playing both offense and defense for Coach Paul "Bear" Bryant at Alabama and his time as head coach at Livingston University and North Alabama provided Coach with the offensive experience he needed to understand what a defensive unit had to do to dominate an offense. He became one of the all-time great defensive coaches not only for FSU, but also in college football. Coach Andrews had an amazing run of All-American defensive backs, coaching two Jim Thorpe Award winners. He also had an All-American cornerback for eight straight years, from 1987 to 1994. So, when Coach Andrews speaks about what it takes to be a great defensive player and defensive team, you listen!

When I asked Coach Andrews what he looked for in a defensive back he replied,

> I want a kid that has mental and physical toughness, who is coachable and will listen to you. I want to see if the kid has the desire and ability to get to the ball carrier and make the tackle or interception. Size and speed are important, but desire and the ability to anticipate the play are critical. A player with desire, mental and

physical toughness, and great anticipation can overcome the lack of great skills.

Coach Andrews added,

> Great defensive players know that every play is important and could be the play that will win or lose the game. They accept accountability and refuse to give up. Most special team players are defensive players and have that attitude. When the players accept accountability and take charge of their team, they will win!

It goes without saying that if a player has what Coach Andrews described it doesn't get any better than that. This sounds like many of the young men that played for Coach Andrews, including Deion Sanders, Terrell Buckley, LeRoy Butler, Clifton Abraham, Corey Sawyer, Tay Cody, and Chris Hope to name a few!

Coach Andrews went on to credit a head coach for setting the tone for a good defensive unit. Coach Andrews and Coach Gladden both praised Coach Bowden for making defense a priority and for the support they got from him to have such success at FSU. Coach Andrews said, "If we were leading at half time, Coach Bowden would tell the defense, "If you don't let them score in the second half, we win the game." He would always challenge us!

Career Defensive Coaches

Coach Jim Gladden and Coach Mickey Andrews both made the decision to be career defensive coaches and stayed with Coach Bowden and FSU for 27 and 26 years respectively. Both value the experience and believe they had the greatest job in the nation, never leaving for other opportunities and possible head coaching roles. They credit Coach Bowden for creating a great environment in which to coach. He trusted them and set a high standard for winning and held them accountable. Coach Bowden said, "If you are looking for a better job then start by making your present job better."

Both coaches make defense sound very basic and compared it to training a bird dog to hunt!

Coach Gladden said, "Coaching a defensive player is like training a hunting dog. If the dog can't do what you are trying to get him to do, let him do what he can do."

Coach Andrews added, "The secret to a good defensive player and team is make them perform like a team of bird dogs that sniff out the birds, flush 'em and then go get them."

Several key thoughts were consistent in my discussions with Coach Bowden, Coach Gladden, and Coach Andrews. Each of them in their own words talked about the team belonging to the players, not the coaches. They each believed that it is the coach's job to hold the players accountable and to make sure they have ownership. "The team belongs to the team!" Each of them discussed skills needed to be successful, but, given the choice of an average player with desire or a great player with little desire, they would take the average player. An average player with the mental and physical toughness will be a player you can depend on! Heart trumps talent!

COACH'S COMMENT

"Coaches Harbison, Gladden, Andrews, and McDowell — I was blessed to have great defensive staff and coaches that I just got out of their way and let them coach. They could really recruit and develop players. They are responsible for the success we had along with the players they recruited and developed." — Coach Bowden

When you put Coach Gladden and Coach Andrews with Coach Harbison and let them coach, you can see why the Seminoles had such a reputation for defense. That is exactly what Coach Bowden did, and the rest is history! Bobby, Jim, Mickey, and Harbie had a great run together and certainly make a Case for the Defense.

PART 3

Seminole Memories

CHAPTER 20
TEAM TAKEAWAYS

Dale McCullers

What have we learned from FSU's defensive players? Life can be very challenging at times. Good health, prosperity, friends and foes, joys, and heartaches all may come and go in an instant or over many decades. Throughout the vicissitudes of life, it seems all of us have obstacles and challenges to overcome. If you think some families or some people are blissfully happy all the time and seem to be void of any significant challenges in life, you probably just don't know them that well.

Over the past five decades we have lost scores of our former 1960s era FSU teammates and coaches. Sadly, these teammates and coaches have gone the way of the whole earth, quietly passing on from this life to the next. While playing football at FSU, some extraordinary people came into my life and left as quickly as they appeared. In our lifetime, most of us usually develop only three to five deep and lasting friendships. However, when any of our closest friends or family members die, symbolically speaking, they seem to just sail on out of sight like a ship moving across the deep ocean and disappearing into the night. Most, if not all, have left this little blue planet with a bright hope of a greater stage of existence somewhere in eternity. The hope is to one day stand together on a much brighter stage, even more wonderful than this mortal journey has been. At this very moment, many of our FSU teammates and coaches are battling life-threatening illnesses and diseases. Unfortunately, many will not be with us much longer.

The golden question we desire to ask our former teammates, coaches, and also our readers, is one with two parts: what can we learn from the game of football, and what can we learn from any person who has accomplished great things in the game of life?

Additionally, what core values do you consider useful after reading the life-long accomplishments of this group of football players and coaches that are chronicled in this book? What have we all learned from the many hundreds of great athletes and coaches, who either played or coached college football across America in the entire past century?

Do you ever take time to ponder some of life's more poignant questions or lessons learned from old friends, teammates, relatives, coaches, teachers, or pastors who have now departed this life? Did their friendships, their examples, their influence, their athletic prowess, or their life's work — as a teammate, a teacher, a friend, or coach — make any lasting impressions on us? Was there anything they ever said, did, or accomplished in their lives that really mattered to those of us who are still living out our lives today?

For the moment, consider just four of our former FSU teammates and our former FSU head coach: Johnny Stephens, (1965-1966 offensive center), Mike Page, (1967 defensive cornerback), Del Williams (1964-1966 offensive tackle and guard), and Chuck Eason (1967-1968 defensive back) and our former FSU Head Coach Bill Peterson.

Shortly after leaving FSU in 1968, 2nd Lieutenant Johnny Stephens was killed in military action during the Vietnam War. In 1968, FSU cornerback Mike Page and his young wife were both killed in a terrible railroad crossing accident during Mike's junior year at FSU. Del Williams, a former FSU All-American guard and a star lineman for the New Orleans Saints, succumbed to Lou Gehrig's disease at age 39 in the prime of his life. A life-long friend and teammate Chuck Eason died earlier this year following a long battle with cancer. Former FSU Head Coach Bill Peterson died in 1993 at the ripe age of 73. To us now living, were the lives of these great football players and the wonderful legacy of Coach Peterson a tragedy or destiny? You decide.

The truth is, even for those of us who knew these teammates and Coach Peterson very well, for the most part, we have likely forgotten many details concerning their individual contributions to FSU football. All I know is, during the 1960s, I personally gained some very valuable insights about the game of football — and the game of life — from Coach Peterson and my fallen FSU teammates.

Each of these players and Coach Pete, in their own unique way and by their own example, left their coaching peers and teammates with many lasting impressions. I remember Coach Pete as a uniquely gifted coach and mentor. I am very grateful I knew Coach Pete personally and played football with Johnny Stephens, Chuck Eason, Mike Page, and Del Williams. I was also very fortunate that Del Williams was a former high school teammate from our shared hometown, Live Oak, Florida. Del was a great football player and a great role model. His example and positive influence were the main reasons I chose to go play college football at FSU.

I think most everyone will agree that the stellar group of FSU Hall of Fame football players and coaches chronicled within this book were very successful in the game of football. What is also remarkable is how successful these players have been in their post collegiate careers. This book has been primarily designed by the authors to recognize and remember an extraordinary group of defensive coaches and athletes who played or coached college football at FSU during the 1960s. Through extensive research and personal interviews, we have come away with a list of common themes, core values, character traits, inspirational concepts, and little gems of wisdom that these extraordinary men have displayed in their lives and shared with us while writing this book.

During our interviews, each of these FSU Athletic Hall of Fame players gave us many inspirational thoughts and wonderful memories of FSU football. In their own unique ways and through their own accomplishments — their words, actions, and their examples — we have found substantial inspiration and great stories that are worth remembering. We felt it may be prudent for our readers to consider some of the gems of wisdom and lessons we learned from these great players, based on some of their common character traits and common core values which they all seemed to exhibit to one degree or another. These core values and character traits seemed to be the driving source, and force, behind their remarkable success stories while playing football and the game of life.

Seven Magnificents: George D'Alessandro, Frank Pennie, Dick Hermann, Jack Shinholser, Bill McDowell, Avery Sumner and Max Wettstein. (Terry Garvin would replace Max Wettstein in 1965 as Max moved to tight end in 1965) Forgotten Four: Maury Bibent, Jim Massey, Winfred Bailey, Howard Ehler.

CHAPTER 21

THE SEVEN MAGNIFICENTS AND THE FORGOTTEN FOUR

John Crowe

The Seven Magnificents and the Forgotten Four represent the theme that Dale and I wanted to capture in our book, recognizing the sons of the Greatest Generation and the Case for the Defense during the 1960s and the Bill Peterson years at FSU. Three members of this group have an individual chapter in our book, and we believe it is fitting to represent them as a team to highlight the importance of their impact on football at FSU. They, along with the Tensi-Biletnikoff aerial circus and talented offense, provided the "breakout year" for the Seminole football program.

The Seven Magnificents is likely the most famed defensive unit in FSU annals. Rated as one of the greatest college football nicknames — along with the Chinese Bandits, the Seven Blocks of Granite, the Red Elephants, and the Four Horsemen — the Seven Magnificents and the Forgotten Four were key to the ascension of Florida State University to the national stage in college football. The front seven got their name in 1964, playing off of the popular 1960 movie "The Magnificent Seven" starring Yul Brynner and Steve McQueen. The Seven Magnificents shaved their heads to emulate Yul Brynner and adopted his persona. Legendary Coach Bob Harbison coached the Seven Magnificents, and they became the standard of what a defense should be.

1964 was the first year that college football rules changed to allow unlimited substitution. This was the beginning of specialization, and for the most part, the end of the days that players would go both ways, playing offense and defense. The Seven Magnificents and the Forgotten Four would start that transition at FSU in a most dominating way, allowing only 66 points in the 10-game regular season. In the first four games that historic year, this hard-hitting band of 11 allowed only one touchdown, and it came when Florida State fumbled a punt reception near its goal.

Like Dale and myself, many of the recruits during this historic season made their decision to come to FSU because of the success of the 1964 Seminoles, highlighted with the first victory over the Florida Gators. In that game, the Florida players had "Go for Seven," (meaning seven victories in a row) on the front of their jerseys; on their practice helmets they wore the inscription: "Never, FSU, Never!" The win over the Gators and the dominating 48-6 win over Kentucky, the #5 team in the nation, were arguably the most important victories in FSU's history. The win over Kentucky is still one of the biggest upsets ever in college football. The icing on the cake that season was the dominating 36-19 victory over the Oklahoma Sooners in the Gator Bowl.

FIRST MEETING WITH THE SEVEN

I remember my first encounter with members of the Seven Magnificents. I was reporting for the 1965 school year, and my parents had just said goodbye to me in front of Salley Hall Dormitory, where the football team and other FSU athletes lived. As I got on the elevator to go to my room on the fourth floor, two men with shaved heads got on the elevator with me. They were wearing cutoff T-shirts that said "Property of FSU Football," shorts and flip flops. I also noticed they had shaved their legs to about their calf muscles. I hadn't seen that before! One of them said to me, "Are you a freshman?" When I answered, "Yes, sir," they both reached down and removed my two suitcases from the elevator and informed me that freshmen use the stairs.

Well, for the next two weeks, even when they weren't present, I used the stairs until I found out they were just kidding. The two players I met that day were George D'Alessandro and Terry Garvin. I would soon run into the rest of the Seven. With their bald heads, they stood out!

THE DRILL I WILL ALWAYS REMEMBER

My first experience with the Seven Magnificents on the field came early in the days to follow. A group of freshmen players were sent to participate in a tackling drill with the Seven where we were to be the ball carrier and target. The defensive player, one of the Seven, would lie on his back with the ball carrier standing with his back turned away from the down player. The coach running the drill would yell "ready, ready" and, as the target, you would do an about-face, and the coach would flip you the football. At the same time, the down lineman would spring off the ground and come to make the tackle. This was a drill to develop quickness. On this particular day, I was second in line and watched as the first freshman player was so quick that he had the ball and delivered a shoulder to the first member of the Seven before he was upright. It was impressive, until coach informed the freshman player that he would need to go again. Needless to say, on his second go at the drill, the Seven were ready for him — and not just one, but three of them.

Being a quick learner, I decided that I would help make the next of the Seven in the drill look good — real good! It just happened to be All-American nose tackle Jack Shinholser. Well, when the coach yelled "ready, ready," I turned to catch the ball, which the coach had thrown 15 feet in the air, and Jack sprang from the ground and reached me with his shoulder in my chest, my arms still reaching for the football. He popped me like a wet noodle. Jack really looked good and received accolades from the coach while I was told to return to the back of the line to wait for another turn. I remember getting up but was unable to straighten up for several minutes while my lungs took their time to inflate again after being squeezed together between Jack Shinholser and the ground. The experience wasn't pretty, but it made a lasting impression — one that has reminded me often that life can be tough, but you can get through it and good times will come if you just learn to be persistent.

CASE FOR THE DEFENSE

I recently had a conversation with a legendary defensive coach, Jim Gladden (1976-2001), about one of the first meetings Bobby Bowden, had with his coaches when he returned in 1976 as the new head coach. Coach Bowden told the coaches that he wanted the fastest and best athletes on defense. The other team couldn't win if they had trouble scoring, and he wanted an offense that wouldn't hurt the defense. Coach Bowden understood a Case for the Defense.

In Peterson's years (1960-1970), he also understood the importance of a strong defense and had a very impressive group of defensive coaches during those years, including Vince Gibson, Don James, Ken Meyer, Bob Harbison, Bobby Jackson, Gary Wyant, Bud Whitehead, and Bill Parcells.

The Seven Magnificents and Forgotten Four are legendary! They will always be spoken of with reverence for the impact they made on FSU football then and today. The seven players who shaved their heads to demonstrate unity to each other and the four who backed them up will always be an outstanding example of what teamwork can deliver. Their teamwork was clearly a lesson for success and a Case for the Defense.

1967 FSU Football Squad
Head Coach: Bill Peterson

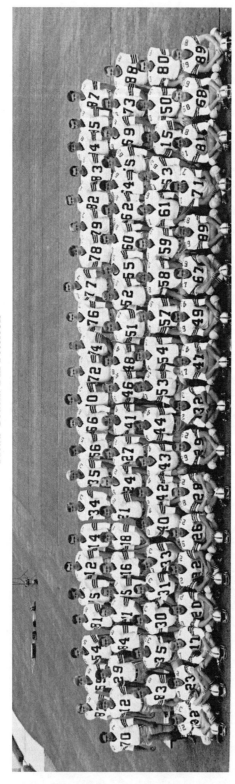

Front Row: Left to Right: Barry Wenhold, Bill Mortiz, Mike Page, Larry Green, Chuck Eason, Hal Hodges, T.K. Wetherell, Chuck Pickens, Ed Chereshkoff, Joe Benson, Terry Eagerton, Mike Bugar, Bob Menendez, Harvey Zion, Phil Abraira, Larry Pendleton, Mike Connors

Second Row: Skip Babbs, John Pittman, Bill Moremen, Bill Gunter, Grant Guthrie, Mike Blatt, Bill Cheshire, Hal Montgomery, Mike Corey, Bobby Burt, Ronnie Montford, Joe Kinnan, Richie Jones, Frank Loner, Chuck Elliott, Richard McLean, Danny Thomas, Dick Johnson, Doug Gurr

Third Row: Tom White, Rick Anderson, Doug Mitchell, Bill Yeldell, Kim Hammond, Tommy Warren, Gary Pajcic, Clint Burton, Donovan Jones, Walt Sumner, Billy Cox, John Crowe, Charlie Huggins, Dale McCullers, Bill Hughes, Wayne McDuffie, Ted Mosley, Barry Rice, Beryl Rice, Stan Walker, Bill Dew, Randy Logan, Duke Johnston, Jerry Jones

Fourth Row: Frank Edmunds, Ed Gibson, Jim Bracken, Jim Tyson, Bill Rhodes, Phil Hiatt, Bill Cappleman, Ron Sellers, Mike Gray, Henry Loshe, Ken Hart, Tony Sewell, Jeff Chapman, Chris Palmer, Jack Fenwick, Jeff Curchin, Wayne Johnson, Frank Vohun, Lane Fenner, Thurston Taylor, Chip Glass, Floyd Ratliff, Jim Rust

CHAPTER 22

1967 — The Comeback Year

John Crowe

A lot was going on in the world in 1967. Protests erupted across the U.S. against the much-maligned Vietnam War. There were also race riots raging in several U.S. cities. Israel fought and won the legendary six-day war against Egypt, Jordan, and Syria. Elvis Presley married Priscilla. The Rolling Stones, the Supremes, and the Beatles dominated the radio airways. America lost three veteran astronauts — Virgil Grissom, Ed White, and Roger Chaffee — when a flash fire occurred during a launch pad test. In Tallahassee, like the other years of the 1960s, the Sons of the Sixties showed up to represent Florida State University on the football field with a very formidable football schedule that included several top ranked teams and programs.

In 1967, the Seminole football team record for the season was 7-2-2. The final results make the 1967 team one of the winningest in FSU history at that time. However, it didn't start out that way. The 1967 FSU football team was young and inexperienced. Of the 85 plus football players who made up the 1967 team roster, 10 were seniors, 25 were juniors, and about 50 were sophomores. Our losses in 1967 were to the University of Houston and North Carolina State, both early in the season. They were both dismal, forgettable games. Bill McGrotha, legendary sports writer for the Tallahassee Democrat, wrote these words about the Houston game:

Under a dark, gray, man-made dome, the roof fell in on Florida State's football team last night. University of Houston's Cougars won the game by a stunning 33-13 score. It might have been somewhat worse.

I believe our first experience indoors and on artificial turf played a factor in our poor performance and responsible for numerous turnovers.

We returned to Tallahassee immediately after the Friday night Houston game in the Astrodome. As Coach Pete would say, "We took a two plane engine home from the game." Practice the following week was a nightmare with practices similar to summer two-a-days. We practiced twice Saturday, after church on Sunday, and had scrimmages Monday through Friday. This was unheard of during the regular season, but it worked. It made a difference, and we were committed to improvement. It showed in our performance the following week with the 37-37 tie against #1 Alabama at Legion Field in Birmingham — in front of the largest crowd the Seminoles had played in front of at that time: 71,299. Bill McGrotha described the effort as the "Greatest Game ever played anywhere." There were many highlights, including outstanding offensive performances by seniors Kim Hammond, Larry Green, Bill Moremen and junior Ron Sellers. Grant Guthrie's perfection on field goals and extra points was critical. On defense, the 75-yard touchdown punt return by Walt Sumner led to Bear Bryant's now famous quote, "What the hell is going on out there?" Chuck Eason's two interceptions were also special! This was one of the early Sod Games,[5] and

5. At FSU, Sod Games and the Sod Cemetery are a rich part of our football history. The tradition was started during the 1960s when Gene McDowell, the captain of the 1962 team, brought home a piece of sod from Sanford Stadium following the 18-0 victory over the favored Georgia Bulldogs. Dean Coyle Moore, long-time professor and member of FSU's athletic board, had issued the challenge to bring back some sod from "between the hedges." As a tribute to victory, Coach Peterson and Dean Moore had the sod buried on the practice field, and the tradition was born. The criteria in those early years was a win or tie in a road game in which Florida State is the underdog. Over the years, it has expanded to include ACC championships, all road games at the University of Florida, and all bowl games. The 1967 team was successful bringing back sod from five games, the most by one team in FSU history. The Sons of the Sixties delivered on 21 Sod Game challenges. Impressive, but then, we were usually the underdog in those days.

we brought home a piece of the turf from Legion Field to bury in the Sod Cemetery. The team returned to Tallahassee to be greeted by a large crowd at the airport. We were flying sky high, and our fans were too! However, a week later we were slammed back to Mother Earth after losing a hard fought game to North Carolina State.

After the 20-10 North Carolina State loss, the following week we trailed 9-0 at half time against Texas A&M in College Station; the outlook was as grim as the rainy sky that day. Things suddenly changed! We pulled out a 19-18 late win following a fumble recovery, and a 28-yard touchdown run by halfback Billy Moremen, capped with a late interception by Walt Sumner. Following the Texas A&M victory, the 1967 team went on to run the table, winning six more games, including our first ever win over the Gators in the Swamp! The closing performance resulted in an invitation to the Gator Bowl to play Penn State. The team again made a late comeback to tie Penn State 17-17 following a defensive stop led by "Knock'em Flat" Mike Blatt on a failed fourth down attempt by Penn State. It was a season of comebacks by a team that believed!

Football is full of 'ifs'. If we had somehow scored just one more point against Alabama in our 37-37 tie and just made one more point in our 17-17 tie against Penn State in the post-season Gator Bowl, our season record would have been 9-2, and our team likely would have been ranked in the top 10 to 12 teams in the nation. As it turned out, we were ranked 15 at the close of the post-season. The saying that a tie is like kissing your sister is overstated. The ties with Alabama and Penn State for the young 1967 football team were special and memorable.

Our turnaround performance in 1967 reflects the growth and development of our young and inexperienced team. During our seven-game win streak, most of our players matured to become seasoned and tested college football veterans. It was a season that verifies the value of having a never-quit attitude and the right leadership. While they were small in number, and maybe small in size compared to today, the 10 seniors had the heart and determination to go from such a poor start to making the team a winner.

On offense, Kim Hammond, Larry Green, Bill Moremen, Thurston Taylor, and Wayne McDuffie were the rocks and foundation; on defense it was "Bobby" Menendez, Mike Blatt, Joe Kinnan, Jerry Jones, and T.K. Wetherell. Our senior players on offense and defense demonstrated leadership by example. They encouraged, inspired, and supported us less experienced under-classmen. A vocal defensive leader in the locker room on game day was defensive end Bob Menendez. Bob could fire up the entire team with his spontaneous Seminole war cry and shouts of acclamation and admonition. I can see him now, standing on the bench waving a towel! A talented senior linebacker, Mike Blatt, quietly demonstrated leadership by his intensity and aggression on the field of play. The two of them along with junior Dale McCullers were the frequent winners of the Savage Award, a weekly honor to the defensive most valuable player. Also a senior leader, T.K. Wetherell always exuded confidence by his quiet but determined demeanor. Our senior players were great mentors and gave their utmost best effort in practice and during games. These young men refused to quit and led the way. They were determined to go out winners! That compliment applies to our coaches who spent hours-upon-hours reviewing film and putting together a winning strategy. However, most successful coaches believe the Team belongs to the Team and they must be accountable. I believe our accountability made a difference and is the reason we went from 0-2-1 to finish at 7-2-2 and Gator Bowl Co-Champions!

On November 3, 2017, the 1967 team was honored by Florida State University to celebrate 50 years since that memorable season. We had a great turnout and fun time remembering the way we were. Many of the Sons of the Sixties from this team had passed by this time. We read each of their names and had a moment of silence in their honor. I will always remember that comeback season we had together and I will forever be proud and grateful to have been part of it.

If any of our readers are interested in a more detailed game-by-game and play-by-play summary of the 1967 FSU football season, we invite you to read "FSU One Time" by Dr. Jim Jones. Jones is a legendary FSU history professor and one of the biggest Seminole fans of all time. In his book, beginning with the early history of FSU football, Dr. Jones provides a masterful analysis of each season and each game throughout the bygone decades of the 1940s, 1950s, and 1960s. More information on the 1967 season in particular can be found on NoleFan.org under the 1967 Year in Review. Legendary Tallahassee Democrat sports writer Bill McGrotha offers a play-by-play analysis of the 1967 football season.

The 1968 Seminoles

THE 1968 SEMINOLES

FIRST ROW—Left to Right: Abraira, Ashmore, Bancroft, Bass, Benson, Bugar, Carrol, Chereshkoff, Crowe, Eagerton, Eason, K. Hughes, H. Montgomery, Page, Pell, Pittman, Thomas, Wenhold, Zion, Corral, Pickens. SECOND ROW—Beville, Davis, Diaz, Elliott, Gildea, Gunter, Gurr, Guthrie, Hall, B. Hughes, Lanahan, Lohse, Loner, Lowe, Munroe, Pederson, Pendleton, Rust, Semanchik, White, Whigham. THIRD ROW—Hipps, Anderson, Bailey, Burt, Burton, Cassady, Cheshire, Cox, Dawson, Jaros, Jarrett, W. Johnson, D. Johnston, Mc Cullers, Mc Eachern, Mosley, Barry Rice, Beryl Rice, Sammons, Sumner, Tyson, Warren, Yeldell, D. Johnson. FOURTH ROW—Cappleman, Curchin, Fenwick, Gaydos, Glass, Gray, Hart, Hiatt, G. Montgomery, Pajcic, Ratliff, Rhodes, Rimby, Sellers, Sewell, Stokes, Strickler, Sykes, Vohun, Walker, Wallace, Mitchell, Logan, Mac Kenzie, Zaffran.

CHAPTER 23

1968 — Seminoles on the War Path

Dale McCullers

F ollowing a respectable 7-2-2 winning season in 1967, all of the coaches, the FSU fan base, and the players themselves had high expectations for the 1968 football season. The team roster was virtually the same as the 1967 roster with a few exceptions. Many of the former underclassmen who returned for the next fall season were now rising junior teammates. At the close of the 1967 season, we lost only four starting defensive players to graduation: defensive ends Bob Menendez and Jerry Jones, linebacker Mike Blatt, and cornerback T.K. Wetherell. Ron Wallace, sophomore, Floyd Ratliff, junior, and Doug Gurr, senior, replaced Menendez and Jones at defensive end; while Joe Benson, senior, and Steve Gildea, sophomore, replaced Mike Blatt. Mike Page, junior, replaced T.K. Wetherell as cornerback.

The starting defensive unit in 1968 included senior linebackers, Joe Benson, Chuck Elliot, and Dale McCullers. Steve Gildea and Mike Bugar were frequent back-ups. Frank Vohun and Harvey Zion were defensive tackles and Ron Wallace, Doug Gurr, and Floyd Ratliff were defensive ends.

The defensive secondary team in frequent rotation included Chuck Eason, Johnny Crowe, Walt Sumner, Howell Montgomery, Clint Burton, John

Pell, and Mike Page. All of these players were rough and ready athletes. Our coaches also did a great job of rotating uniquely talented younger players as frequent back-ups during games. This timely and regular substitution of these excellent defensive players helped our defense maintain intensity and reduce fatigue.

I remember several games when the temperature on the field was in the high 90s. The humidity was so bad in a few games I felt like I was inhaling warm water instead of muggy air. While playing our rival Florida in both 1967 and 1968, some players lost up to 15 to 17 pounds during the game. This was due to high intensity of a rivalry game and high temperatures on the field of play. One of our stellar receivers, Billy Cox, lost 17 pounds in a game in the infamous Swamp in Gainesville. In that same game, I lost 14 pounds. The average fan has no idea how physically taxing four quarters of football can be sometimes. Even though we routinely digested salt pills before playing on hot days, quite a few players had serious dehydration problems and leg cramps. A few players routinely had leg cramps long after the game was over. We survived it.

We had a great bunch of defensive linemen and linebackers and a superb defensive secondary. Hal Montgomery, Clint Burton, and John Pell had frequent back-up duty for the starting secondary. Steve Gildea, Bobby Burt, Theron Bass, and Mike Bugar filled in for the starting linebacker corps; and Duke Johnston and Robert McEachern filled in at defensive tackle for Vohun and Zion.

All of these players were superbly capable teammates in both the starting line-up and back-up roles. The only real difference between our starters and the back-ups was less playing time and game experience. Three of our senior substitute players were also dealing with serious knee injuries: Mike Bugar, Doug Gurr, and Hal Montgomery had undergone knee surgery early in their collegiate careers. Prior to their knee injuries, all three of these players could have been in a starting line-up anywhere in the nation. Although these knee injuries had left all of them with reduced flexibility, none of them reduced their aggressive style of play. I always quietly admired these three senior players for their unselfish attitudes and their unwavering commitment to do what they could do to support their younger or less-experienced teammates.

Our team record was a respectable 8-2 during the regular season. We hoped for an undefeated season, but the Florida game took some of the air out of our proverbial sail. Our third loss happened in the post-season, at the Peach Bowl against LSU. We lost that game by a small margin of 4 points, 31-27, in a hard-fought gridiron battle. All of our opponents were tough competitors, but Virginia Tech, Florida, LSU, and Houston also had exceptional teams in 1968. Consistently winning football games is not an easy task at the college and pro level, as players are routinely challenged by talented athletes on the opposing teams. Our eight wins were exhilarating and fun. Our three losses were a mixture of just getting beat by our opponent and too many costly mistakes or penalties. However, we were a resilient group of hard-nosed Seminoles. We didn't quit until the final whistle blew. Our unspoken promise was that if we did get beat on the scoreboard, our opponent would feel they paid for the price of victory in their bruised bodies.

As stated earlier, we had high hopes of an undefeated season, but that dream quickly dissipated when our nine-game winning streak came to an abrupt end against the Florida Gators. In our second game of the season, we lost to the Gators in a hard-fought defensive battle. There was no love lost between the Seminoles and the Gators. To be honest, it was an emotion of intense dislike, mingled with competitive respect. I admit the rivalry has been good for each school, generating revenue and national recognition for both teams. The rivalry has made each program better and proves you get better if you face great competition! However, I have family members who are big Gator fans, so I have to exercise restraint and bite my tongue at reunions. You would think that at age 70, I would be willing to now extend the olive branch in peace. Well, maybe — time will tell.

After soundly defeating Maryland 24-14 in our season opener, our usually potent offense was "woefully pitiful," as characterized by Tallahassee Democrat sports writer Bill McGrotha in his post-game sports column. This was the first time FSU had not scored a touchdown since North Carolina State beat FSU 3-0 in 1965. In the loss to Florida, the FSU defense was terrific, but the monumental defensive effort was somewhat overlooked. A great offense sells tickets, but a great defense is what keeps college and pro teams in the hunt for championships. If your opponent can't score, your chances of winning the game are dramatically increased. Despite the loss to Florida, there were some defensive highlights. As a senior linebacker, I made 26 tackles (18 unassisted and eight assisted) in the losing effort.

Safety Johnny Crowe made 13 tackles and one interception in the Florida game. Sophomore linebacker Steve Gildea made nine tackles, and defensive back Hal Montgomery made an interception in the game. Defensive tackles Harvey Zion and Frank Vohun did a great job of rushing the quarterback all game, and defensive ends Ron Wallace and Floyd Ratliff created havoc on the edges with their aggressive style of play. Defensive backs Walt Sumner, Johnny Crowe, Mike Page, John Pell, Hal Montgomery, Clint Burton, and Chuck Eason repeatedly covered Florida receivers like a proverbial blanket. The Gator passing attack, so used to piling up big yardage against opponents in the passing game, could only muster 162 yards in the air. Our defensive line stymied Florida's offense time and time again. The problem was clearly the lack of offense on both sides of the ball. Florida's All-American running back Larry Smith gained only 62 yards. Neither team could score effectively throughout the game. It was Florida's defensive effort that was the key in winning the game. The final score was 9-3. It was a sloppy win by Florida, and a poor offensive display by FSU on our home field.

One of the things you learn as a football player is to get over tough losses quickly and move on. The physical and emotional pain is sometimes difficult to absorb, more difficult for some than others. We were a resilient bunch, so we just worked hard to improve, and we all strived to have short memories. Our hard work and forgetfulness paid off. We had three wins in a row over Texas A&M, Memphis State, and South Carolina. Our offense started clicking on all cylinders. During these three wins, our offense was exceptional. Our defense performed equally as well during all three back-to-back wins. Our pass defense was one of the best in the nation with 25 interceptions in 1968.

Johnny Crowe and Walt Sumner were the clear leaders in the secondary team, making 5 interceptions each in the 1968 season. These two guys were exceptionally talented players. The average fan does not realize how difficult it is to make just one interception on the college or pro level. It requires split second timing, agility, and aggressively going for the football. Add to the equation the receiver knowing his precise route and premeditated cuts or moves, while the defender is left only to react to the receiver's movements. I have no idea how our superb defensive secondary team covered so many speedy and elusive receivers, game after game, without making any major mistakes, getting beat deep very often, or committing costly penalties. The truth is, they were probably the most prepared secondary in the nation. Coach Gary Wyant was relentless in watching game film, demanding perfection and getting the very best out of his defensive backs.

Our secondary was nicknamed the Rat Pack. This moniker was perfect. They were all a little under-sized and under-weight, but certainly not under the radar. They were everywhere on the field. They swarmed to the ball carrier or receiver like a "pack of rats" with ravenous appetites. All of them were tough as nails. None of them would shy away from making a hit on a ball carrier at full speed. The Rat Pack had plenty of game experience. Our team had five seniors in the secondary who had lettered in their sophomore, junior, and senior years: Sumner, Crowe, Eason, Burton, and Montgomery. Page and Pell were the underclassmen sharing starting duty at right corner in 1968. The Seminole defense held opponents to only 139 passing yards on the average per game. Our opponents scored only 10 touchdown passes the entire season. This equates to giving up just one touchdown in the air per game.

The Rat Pack had individual nicknames and a mouse logo on their team jacket. Their nicknames were:

Coach Gary Wyant — Daddy Rat

Senior Corner Walt Sumner — Lightning Rat

Senior Safety Johnny Crowe — Skinny Rat

Senior Safety Chuck Eason — Thunder Rat

Senior Safety Clint Burton — Splinter Rat

Senior Safety Hal Montgomery — Mumbles Rat

Junior Corner Mike Page — Little Rat

Junior Corner John Pell — Speedy Rat

Junior Corner Danny Thomas — No Name Rat

The Rat Pack was a close group and unit! They were like a pack of wolves, only smaller!

The linebackers complemented the Rat Pack. Our linebackers contributed to an amazing seven aerial picks during the 1968 season. It is also remarkable that 11 defensive players made one interception or more during the season. The FSU interception rate was well over two interceptions per game, an outstanding achievement. This included four interceptions in one game against All-American quarterback Ed Hargett in our win over Texas A&M.

I have a great deal of respect for my fellow linebackers. Joe Benson and Chuck Elliott were two very talented and smart linebackers. I admit they were smarter than me. Chuck and Joe will verify I was certifiably crazy about getting to the football, going through or around friend or foe.

Continuing our season summary, after achieving three wins in a row against Texas A&M, Memphis State, and South Carolina, our team experienced a rude awakening against Virginia Tech in Tallahassee on our home field. The previous year, our team had soundly trounced Virginia Tech 38-15 in another home game. Our opponent was out for revenge, and they certainly got it. They gave us a 40-20 shellacking. There was an extraordinary amount of trash talk on the field by a few Virginia Tech players and a few Seminoles who chose to respond. Fifty years later, I still sadly reflect on this terrible loss, and the early season loss against the Gators. Losses are particularly tough when you get bad breaks in the game or too many costly penalties. What is the hardest to swallow is when your best effort in a game was just not good enough to win. However, not to wallow in self-pity, or to accept mediocrity again, our team rebounded and won four straight games against Mississippi State, North Carolina State, Wake Forest, and Houston.

Some interesting notes about the Houston game, the previous weekend Houston had defeated Tulsa University with a whopping score of 100-6. In all the news outlets in Tallahassee, and reportedly in Houston, all the sports writers were giving us "no chance" to win. Coach Pete used the psychological ploy of telling all the news outlets the upcoming game against Houston was a "complete mismatch." He also told us in a team meeting that we were "clearly outmatched" against Houston. This statement roused our collective animosity toward the Houston Cougars. We were not happy with Coach Pete making this statement about us not being up to the task of possibly winning the upcoming game. It helped us to develop a higher level of pride in being more competitive than we had in earlier losses. We were determined to shock the world and beat Houston soundly. I recall everyone had razor-sharp instincts in the game. We were also relaxed with virtually no pre-game anxiety because all the pressure was on Houston. We were not expected to win, so we just had fun in the game. Another ploy by Coach Pete was to have us wear our dirty practice jerseys. He gave the options to change into fresh jerseys following warm-ups, but we declined. The ploys by Coach Pete and our renewed energy to prevail worked.

In late November, in a neutral-site night game in Jacksonville, Florida, our high-powered offense came of age and scored 40 points on a very surprised Houston team. They underestimated the strong competitive spirit of their opponent. Our defense held Houston to only 20 points, when their game average was over 40 plus points per game. Houston's last touchdown was late in the game after the starting defense was celebrating on the sideline. Our younger back-up teammates were able to play two or three series of downs toward the end of the game. The following week our team received an invitation to play in the post-season Peach Bowl against LSU. Our season record was 8-2, and we ended up ranked 14th in the final UPI poll.

1968 was a great year to be a Florida State Seminole. Our graduating seniors and younger teammates overcame adversity, many bumps, bruises, and injuries, and demoralizing setbacks. However, we still ended up winners in every respect. I suppose the greatest lesson all of us young men learned in the 1968 season was to never quit. We also learned to believe in one another. In summary, we learned when you perform at your highest level, good things happen. We all learned to have unwavering confidence in hard work, mental toughness, teamwork, and preparation as sure foundation stones to reap the rewards of success in life.

Fifty years after our FSU football experience, many of our former teammates at class reunions express over and over again their immense gratitude to have once been a Seminole football player and to wear the garnet and gold uniform. We are grateful for our athletic scholarships that helped many of us get an education we could not otherwise have afforded. As we look back in time to the 1967 to 1968 era of Seminole football, there are feelings of nostalgia, great satisfaction, a few regrets, a sense of pride and belonging, but most of all a deep sense of pure gratitude. We are grateful for our parents, all members of the Greatest Generation. They gave us some opportunities in life they never had. We are the Sons of the Sixties, also known as the baby boomers. We are the children of those men and women who persevered and endured the Great Depression and World War II. In the end, they not only prevailed, but they excelled as superb parental role models, despite overcoming immense odds and extreme hardship. We are grateful for our Seminole fans and our coaches and college professors who supported us and helped us find our place in the world. Finally, we are especially grateful to our Seminole teammates who worked and worked, and sometimes hurt, alongside us in grueling practices and highly competitive football games. These Seminole players of our youth still remain in our old age, a true and faithful band of Seminole brothers. We are family.

CHAPTER 24
LEST WE FORGET

By Dale McCullers

Throughout human history there are many men and women who have paid the ultimate sacrifice by giving their lives in defense of country, friends, or family. Thus, as the profoundly timeless proverb in holy writ states: "Greater love hath no man than this, that a man lay down his life for his friends" (John 15:13)

In 2003, Judge James "Jim" Joanos, a highly respected FSU alumnus and and FSU Athletic Hall of Fame Inductee, used these same apostolic words in the opening line of an article written by him for the Seminole Boosters about 2nd Lieutenant Johnnie P. Stephens Jr. Tragically, after graduating from FSU in 1967, Johnnie was killed during military action while on patrol near the village of Duc Tan, South Vietnam, almost 50 years ago on April 22, 1969. He died in a foreign land far from home and family. He was only 23 years old. To those who knew Johnnie well, he will always be admired. He is not, and will not be, forgotten by his friends, and especially by his loving family. For those readers who may not know much about Johnnie Stephens, in the article by Judge Joanos (who is a retired Chief Judge of the Florida First District Court of Appeals in Tallahassee, Florida), he wrote a masterful biographical sketch about Johnnie's early family life and his stand-out football career at FSU from 1963 to 1966. It also contains many interesting stories about the 1964-66 era of Seminole football, plus many valuable insights about Johnnie's noble character. This article is titled

"An American Hero — Johnnie P. Stephens Jr." In brief, during Johnnie's collegiate career, he was a superb offensive center for the Seminoles. He was also a talented long snapper for the team. Coaches and teammates knew him as an "Iron-Man" for playing every single down throughout the entire 1965 football season. This is a feat that reportedly has not been duplicated in the history of FSU football.

Johnny Crowe and I, the co-authors of this book, were freshman and sophomore teammates of Johnnie Stephens during the 1965 and 1966 seasons, when Johnnie was the starting offensive center for the Seminoles. We both can attest that Johnnie was a hard worker, a hard-nosed football player, and a consummate team player. Johnnie was also a great role model for the younger and more impressible athletes on the team. He was kind, unselfish, thoughtful of others, and of strong moral character. Although he was undersized for an offensive center, he possessed true grit. He was also a highly disciplined athlete, possessing an exceptional work ethic. He was determined to fulfill his assigned role to deliver the football with exactness, and on time, to the quarterback. Johnnie perfected the art of being a long snapper for the Seminoles by demanding perfection of himself. It was not unusual to see Johnnie working on his delivery of a football, repeatedly snapping the ball to an imaginary quarterback or place kicker, long after practice ended. Johnnie believed "perfect practice makes perfect." When the news of him being mortally wounded on patrol in Vietnam got to his teammates, it was like a giant oak tree had fallen in our midst. Johnnie was loved and admired. His kind expression, exceptional work ethic, and his devotion to God, friends, family, and country will never be erased in the memories of those who knew and loved him.

COACH'S COMMENT   "A tough and scrappy kid! He deserves recognition for his contributions to FSU and for his sacrifice defending our country." — Coach Bowden

Johnnie was the type of person who would shy away from wearing the "hero mantle" or characterizing himself as a "hero." Johnnie would likely mention others as being more worthy recipients of such an honor. Nevertheless, Johnnie is a true American hero to his teammates, coaches, family, and friends.

In addition to Johnnie's ultimate sacrifice and legacy as a football player and soldier, there are also many of our 1965-1969 era teammates who are also now deceased. All were very special people. Many were great role models for their coaches and teammates. Furthermore, scores of former teammates are now in poor health. Many more may also leave us in the not so distant future. Cited below is a list of our 1965-1969 era fellow teammates, coaches, and FSU football administrative staff members who are now deceased. We feel all of these great men or teammates are certainly worthy to be recognized as good and decent men who all made significant contributions to FSU football.

Our Seminole Teammates —
1965-1969 Era Memorial List

Phil Abraira, E	*Terry Garvin, DE*	*Tony Sewell, DL*
Tom Bailey, RB	*Mike Gray, E*	*Johnnie Stephens, C*
Maury Bibent, DB	*Billy Gunter, RB*	*Larry Strickland, LB*
Dave Braggins, DL	*Kim Hammond, QB*	*Donn Szaro, DE*
Clint Burton, DB	*Donovan Jones, RB*	*Thurston Taylor, E*
Chuck Calhoun, T	*Wayne McDuffie, OL*	*Bob Urich, OL*
Jeff Chapman, P	*Billy Moremen, RB*	*T. K. Wetherell, DB*
Mike Connors, DB	*Mike Page, DB*	*Max Wettstein, E*
Pat Conway, DB	*Gary Pajcic, QB*	*Del Williams, OL*
Jeff Curchin, OL	*Calvin Patterson, RB*	
Chuck Eason, DB	*Floyd Ratliff, DE*	

Coaches and Administrative Staff—
1965-1969 Era Memorial List

Al Conover, Assistant Coach

Tillman Dixon, Equipment Manager

Don Fauls, Head Trainer

Doug Hafner, Chief Recruiter

Vaughn Mancha, Athletic Director

Bill Peterson, Head Coach

Neil Schmidt, Assistant Coach

Note: If we have omitted any deceased 1960s era teammates/coaches, it is because no information was available to identify and recognize them at printing deadline.

Reflecting on the loss of our many teammates, associates, coaches, and also many of the parents of the Greatest Generation previously cited in this book, we all seem to find comfort for our grief in various ways. The great poet William Wordsworth captured a beautiful sentiment with these stirring poetic lines, which may be helpful in dealing with our loss in his "Ode — Intimations of Immortality," as follows:

> Our birth is but a sleep and a forgetting, the Soul that rises with us our life's star / Hath had elsewhere its setting, and cometh from afar / Not in entire forgetfulness, and not in utter nakedness, but trailing clouds of glory, do we come, from God, who is our home.

In closing out this chapter, we, as co-authors of this book, are eternally grateful for our own deceased parents, and the many noble parents who were known collectively as the Greatest Generation. Like many great generations of the past, it is our hope there will be many exceedingly greater generations from the future that will make many positive and uplifting contributions to the world in general.

We are also grateful for all of our Seminole teammates and coaches like Johnnie Stephens, Del Williams, Coach Peterson, Clint Burton, Gary Pajcic, Kim Hammond, Chuck Eason, and many others mentioned on our memorial list who are now fallen, but not forgotten. They remain our comrades, friends, coaches, or teammates. To us now living, they will always be our unforgotten heroes and friends.

Closing Arguments

JOHN CROWE - FSU DEFENSIVE BACK 1965-1968

First, if you are reading this closing argument, then we were successful in getting "FSU's Sons of the Sixties: A Case for the Defense" published. Regardless, the effort was valuable to Dale and me, and the experience was special. I will always remember the time I spent with the players and coaches who graciously shared their thoughts with me about our theme and what it takes to be successful as a defensive player, a team, and in your life pursuits. The time I spent on this project brought back so many memories of family, teammates, and coaches that made a difference in my life. I will always be thankful that Dale was persistent in his push to work together on this. Dale and I were teammates and friends in college, but with this effort we have become bonded brothers!

Now, to make my final argument for our thesis. The boys, the men about whom we have written are all sons of parents who were part of the Greatest Generation and raised their children to have a strong faith, love of country, consistent work ethic, polite manners, and appropriate toughness — both mental and physical. Each of us grew up in a meager, but loving environment at a time when the family unit was the base and foundation. The 1960s were a confusing time in our history, starting with a new wave of music and the Beatles and ending with Neil Armstrong walking on the moon. The decade had the controversy of the Vietnam War and the assassinations of President Kennedy, Bobby Kennedy, and Martin Luther King, Jr. It was a time of change and transition.

Coach Gladden shared a comment in his interview that I found to be true about families in the 1960s: "During times of confusion and adversity, the defensive team would always insist we go back to our 'base' defense and regain stability." I realized that like in football, having a "base" to go back to during difficult situations in life's journey was key to dealing with problems and not giving up. There are many phrases that people use to describe this, and you have heard a few: "When the going gets tough, the tough get going," "It is always too soon to quit," "You have to hurt a little to get better," "Hang together," "Never, never, never give up," and, one of my favorites, "When God closes one door, he opens another." I used to think those words were in the Bible, but my preacher informed me otherwise; however, they should be! The players and coaches we covered in our book understood the value of a game plan for a football game — and one for life.

Dale and I owe Florida State University more than we can ever repay. We earned a quality education and had opportunities that our parents didn't have. We developed a level of both mental and physical toughness from playing defensive football that served us well throughout our careers. This is exactly what we heard from each of the players and coaches we wrote about, and we believe most of our teammates would say the same. Defensive football, like life, is full of uncertainty; it requires a person to analyze and react. Having a strong base with values and experience will make the difference in how you respond. The training we received by playing defense for the Seminoles made a positive impact in our lives.

While working for Procter and Gamble, I was fortunate to have a boss that recommended I attend a leadership seminar hosted by Steven Covey. Mr. Covey studied successful leaders and summarized his findings in a best-selling book, "Seven Habits of Highly Effective People." He discovered that the first habit of all great leaders is to begin with the end in mind. All great athletes understand this habit. High jumpers and pole vaulters see themselves clearing the bar before they approach the takeoff point. Mr. Covey had us write our personal mission statement. Actually, he had us plan our own funeral. What would we want people to say about us at the end of our life? The key learnings for me were to anticipate, envision, and have a life plan. Write it down and read it to yourself often. Believe good things will happen, and they will! The saying "If you don't know where you are going, you will get nowhere!" is correct. The players, teammates and coaches in our book had a game plan for life, and they executed!

I believe in the power of role models, and many of those whom we highlighted were among my earliest. Watching the Seven Magnificents and the Forgotten Four play team defense in 1964 made me want to come to FSU and be a part of it. My parents were role models, and I found that to be a common feeling among those featured in our book. Our parents instilled values in us that made us persistent and mentally tough. Have you ever noticed how children walk like their parents? I believe it comes from holding your parents' hand as a child. Role models are important in football and in life — be one!

Another common trait held by the characters of our book was a strong work ethic. Each of these people grew up working very labor-intensive jobs. From working in lumber mills to farming, the early lessons carried over into how we practiced and played. I have heard people say, work smart, not hard. I say do both. Let me give you an example.

Cal Ripkin, Jr., the Baseball Hall of Fame great, was a role model for me. He worked hard and smart. He played in 2,632 consecutive games and was known as the Iron Man! When asked about the record, he said that he didn't set out to break Lou Gehrig's record, he just did what his dad told him to do: "Show up dressed and ready to play every day — and play well!" The defensive players and coaches we have represented in this book had that Iron Man trait and always showed up dressed and ready to play, both in football and in life!

Each player and coach put in the hours to develop their skills and be prepared. Each was willing to do more than the minimum requirement to be better as a player, coach, and professional. I learned this lesson early from my math classes in high school. Did you ever wonder why the teacher didn't assign the even problems in a math book? That is because the answers were not in the back of the book like the odd problems were. I decided to work the even problems also, and it paid off. At test time, guess where the questions came from? That's right, from the even problems! It is that way in life; the test comes from doing what isn't assigned. Doing more than the minimum and what others aren't willing to do will improve your performance. You may not receive immediate payback or instant reward, but you will get the opportunities when they come your way. And when you do, some people will describe you as lucky, but luck is just meeting opportunity with preparedness. The Sons of the Sixties understood this principle and did more than the minimum — they did the even problems, as well! Defensive football is all about team effort, and to be successful a player depends on the performance of those around him. The lessons learned playing defensive football at FSU carried into the careers of the Sons of the Sixties. Each person learned the importance of teamwork and being a team player. You must play your position in harmony with your teammates and have interdependency upon one another. In life, like in football, seldom is anything of significant importance achieved by one person.

The Sons of the Sixties are now in the fourth quarter of their life plans. We know this because the IRS makes us take a Required Minimum Distribution, RMD, from our IRAs so they can get all the taxes before our plans expire. Looking back on the first three quarters of my life, I feel blessed to have had the experience of playing defensive back at Florida State University and being a Seminole. It prepared me to deal with whatever life's journey presented me. The Sons of the Sixties had an edge when it came to dealing with a problem situation because of the lessons learned about ourselves playing defensive football, knowing they could reach a little deeper and go a little further than the competition.

In the interviews I conducted, I found gentle and humble men. I thought it remarkable that each had the physical and mental toughness it took to be successful as a defensive performer and to achieve success in their careers, and yet, I would describe their leadership styles and manner as bold with humility. They got it done and didn't have to brag about it. They were humble about their achievements but not boastful, and each had, and still has, a gentle and caring toughness!

The Sons of the Sixties we highlighted in our book fulfilled the dreams their parents had for them using their athletic abilities to earn a scholarship and graduate from Florida State University. Today, all are avid Seminole supporters and a credit to FSU. It has been my honor to document their stories, and many times during the process, I have had a tear of respect and joy in my eye. That is my closing argument for the Sons of the Sixties and a Case for the Defense! To all of them I say, "Well done!"

DALE MCCULLERS - FSU LINEBACKER 1965-1968

My Case for the Defense and closing argument is based on experiences as a high school, college, and professional linebacker. To put my feelings about being a Seminole football player over 50 years ago into words — reflecting from the vantage point of my early 70s — I still feel immense joy and pride to have once played for FSU. I have sincere appreciation for the valuable insights and great memories I gained at FSU while wearing the garnet and gold uniform. During the 1960s, a bygone decade, I feel that I came of age, becoming more grateful, more mature, and a more responsible American citizen. I believe this soul growth happened because I learned to make uncommon sacrifices, to maintain a positive attitude, and to keep steady hands-to-the-plow mentality and work ethic. I found out hard work never killed anybody, but it can hurt pretty bad. However, I must admit there is great fellowship in suffering for a greater cause than my own selfish aspirations; it brings forth blessings from heaven, it increases your self-esteem, helps you love your fellow man, and it helps you gain empathy and respect for the life challenges of other people.

My Case for Defense is joyfully emotional. It is sincere. Cited below are some of my deepest thoughts about what football meant to me as a young man. My feelings about once being a Florida State Seminole football player are pretty simple. I have found nothing in life so far — except for my love of God, family, and country — that compares to being a college athlete. I simply loved the competitive nature of the game. Nothing in life has been more exhilarating, more gratifying, or more fun than playing college football at FSU. That is, except for the lifelong joy of being married to my high school sweetheart, raising four children, spoiling eight grandchildren, and staying loyal to my upbringing and moral convictions. There is nothing I would redo, trade, or compromise for just having the opportunity to play football for the Florida State Seminoles — with some of the best teammates on the planet, I might add. Most of my Seminole teammates feel the same way.

I have pondered, since I took on co-authoring this book, why was I so over-the-top passionate about FSU football as a young man. Without hesitation, I can share with you my unabashed feelings as a defensive linebacker at FSU. I hope these innermost thoughts and feelings will convince you that my Case for the Defense has merit.

A lot of athletes think they would like to know the final outcome of a fiercely competitive gridiron contest before the battle begins. Not me. I never wanted to eliminate the challenges associated with the unknown, meaning that the final outcome was clearly decided by the fight in the dog on the football field. Unless you are a prophet, seer, and revelator, merely wishing, hoping, talking big, pontificating, and predicting makes little sense to me and usually does not affect the final scoreboard on game day. It may fuel the rivalry or enhance love for the game, but it will not help the football player execute his assignments with the required toughness and precision needed to win the game. Football players do not know the outcome of the game until they know it. We all find out by looking at the scoreboard as the playing time runs out.

Most football players strive to be aggressively passionate on the football field. We all strive to use our God-given agency and talents to make a positive contribution to the team's united effort to win the game. Again, with an eye of faith, self-confidence, and team unity, when the game starts, football players venture into the unknown, meaning they have to step a few steps into the dark, ready or not, as they confront the enemy. Similar in some ways to a combat soldier, football players do not know if they will win or not. Although it is not a life and death situation, the emotions are much like an infantry soldier, excluding the fear of death. A football player must step up and be counted, so to speak, boldly fighting and persevering until the final whistle blows. Football players want to win every game, against all opponents, but they do not know beforehand the sacrifice that will be required to actually win the battle. Like a soldier, a football player has to often muster some uncommon courage to fight through heat exhaustion and pain, to believe in their preparation and training, and to "give it their all." Great football players fully believe their training and true grit effort will prevail.

Most defensive players during the 1960s believed their hard work and training would not fail them. Unfortunately, it sometimes did. They also believed their intense will to succeed would be rewarded more often than not. To a defensive player who rarely got the chance to score a touchdown, playing at a high level of intensity and giving your best effort was the ultimate joy, win or lose. Losing a game temporarily affects the ego, but not for long. Believe it or not, most players get over losses quicker than fans or coaches. Negative "poor me" energy never helps. If a defensive player did his best to defend his goal and keep the opponent from scoring, the onus is on the offense to win the game. The truth is, it's easier to score touchdowns than defend your team's goal. That's why great coaches put some of their fastest and toughest athletes on defense. Ask Coach Bobby Bowden or Coach Bob Harbison. You have to remember the offense knows the play, snap count, scheme, and pre-planned leverage, while the defense is left to react. The offense clearly has the advantage in my opinion. The only problem is, I have a high opinion of my opinion. It doesn't get any better for a defensive unit to stop an opponent cold than when it is third down and inches to go. Great defensive teams and great defensive players seem to always find a way to stop the opponent during crucial moments in the game.

A defensive player gets the thrill often to throw caution to the wind, using their reactionary skill, and to engage the opponent with fury and reckless abandon. My Case for the Defense is essentially that it is more fun, more rewarding, and more liberating than playing offense. I have played both offense and defense in high school, college, and as a pro, so I have a different perspective between offense and defense. You need both to win games, but a defensive player can use all of his primal instincts without thinking too much about protecting the football, passing, receiving, or handling the football, or dealing with the pressure to score points, except while advancing an offensive fumble or defensive interception. A defensive player can just line up properly and aggressively hit one, two, or maybe even three opponents while getting to the ball carrier. In brief, it is legally sanctioned to get to a ball carrier with reckless abandon, "go crazy," and hit the ball carrier so hard they likely may feel faint or nauseous — or both. It sounds sadistic, but football is a contact sport. It is just great therapy if you're tense or frustrated.

It is somewhat odd, but to exert yourself well beyond your comfort level, to sweat profusely, and to use all of your might, and a little bit of soul to fight a strong-willed antagonist, but the reward is a natural high. To kindle the fire within is a great reward for a defensive player: your soul seems to grow even in a loss. When you give your best and it's still not good enough, it feels like you have been driven to your knees in adversity. However, overcoming resistance, tough losses, and opposition make you stronger; you must get off your knees and keep fighting. Defensive football has helped me and countless others endure tough times and prevail over adversity and opposition in life. It is strange, but pushing and pulling against opposition or resistance is what actually propels you forward and gives you joy in the end. This is particularly so in the fourth quarter of a football game!

Great defensive players never quit; they just keep chopping wood and stoking the fire within.

FSU's Sons of the Sixties: A Case for the Offense

John Crowe

This chapter was an add-on following our initial completion of our writings. In football terms, you would say we called an audible or changed the play. Dale and I focused on defense when writing our book. We included 12 defensive players. By coincidence, there were 12 offensive players from the 1960s in the FSU Athletic Hall of Fame. We believe we should recognize them and mention a few more of FSU's Sons of the Sixties.

If we had written a book entitled "FSU's Sons of the Sixties: A Case for the Offense," the chapters would be named for the following standouts:

1. Steve Tensi, QB

2. Fred Biletnikoff, WR

3. Bill "Red" Dawson, End

4. Del Williams, G

5. Kim Hammond, QB

6. Wayne McDuffie, G and Coach

7. Ron Sellers, WR

8. Gary Pajcic, QB

9. Larry Pendleton, G and Coach

10. Billy Rhodes, OT

11. Bill Cappleman, QB

12. Rhett Dawson, WR

I am sure you recognize most of these names and remember them for some great memories during the 1960s. Fred Biletnikoff, Red Dawson, Wayne McDuffie, and Larry Pendleton played defense until crossing over to the dark side (just kidding). For many years, Fred's 99-yard interception returned for a touchdown against Miami in 1963 was the longest return in FSU football history.

Fred Biletnikoff and Ron Sellers were both first team All-Americans and were the first two to have their numbers retired, #25 and #34. Fred is in the Pro-Football Hall of Fame, and Ron is in the College Football Hall of Fame. Tensi, Biletnikoff, the Dawson Brothers, Williams, Hammond, Sellers, Rhodes, and Cappleman all played professional football in the NFL. Wayne McDuffie coached for the Atlanta Falcons, the University of Georgia, and at Florida State University. Larry Pendleton started in 33 straight games — an iron man!

Many brothers have played at FSU, but the Dawson brothers are the only two to be in the FSU Athletic Hall of Fame together. The redheads from Valdosta were standout performers and team leaders. Red Dawson has written a book about his experience at Marshall and the tragic airplane crash that took the lives of the Marshall team and coaches in 1970.

It was interesting to me that two positions are notably missing from the FSU Athletic Hall of Fame during this era: running backs and defensive tackles. Why is that? I pondered the question and came to the conclusion that because of the emphasis on the passing game, the running backs had a hidden role and tackles have to be exceptional to get a highlight. Could that be because blocking is not exciting? There were many great running backs in the 1960s, and I am sure you will recognize their names and can maybe recall their achievements: Keith Kinderman, Dave Snyder, Marion Roberts, Wayne Giardino, Phil Spooner, Jim Mankins, Bill Moremen, Larry Green, Bill Gunter, and Tom Bailey.

The era had some great performers at quarterback, and Eddie Feely and Ed Pritchett deserve recognition with the four listed above.

The offensive tackles and guards that deserve mention: Don Donatelli, Jerry Brunner, Tom West, Ed Pope, Dave Braggins, Larry Kissam, Jack Fenwick, Stanley Walker, and Jeff Curchin.

In closing, I would like to return to the defense and recognize some outstanding defensive tackles: Frank Pennie, Avery Sumner, Charlie Pennie, Frank Vohun, Harvey Zion, and Robert McEachern.

Finally, we know that we have missed many FSU Sons of the Sixties who performed well for the FSU Seminoles and we apologize to them. Two names that often came up during our discussions with coaches were the two outstanding defensive players from Key West, Florida — Bobby Menendez and Mike Blatt. Coaches Jackson and Wyant assumed those two were in the FSU Athletic Hall of Fame already, and they deserve to be. Both were team leaders and terrific defensive performers! Excuse the pun, but they are FSU Athletic Hall of Famers in my book!

There is a great opportunity for a book to make a Case for the Offense! I hope somebody will. Dale and I would be glad to help.

ACKNOWLEDGMENTS

Recognizing those who have contributed to our book is a pleasure but creates the risk that we might miss someone. We would like to start by thanking the players and coaches that made the book possible by their contributions to FSU as athletes, coaches, and for their accomplishments in their diverse careers. Each graciously helped us by making time for interviews and phone calls.

We appreciate the professionals at FSU that helped us complete the project — Charlie Barnes, Rob Wilson, Katie Pugh, and Sue Hall. Bob Perrone's creation of the website NoleFan.org was a great resource. As a Seminole fan, you need to check out this website — it's awesome!

We want to thank the Florida State University Athletic Hall of Fame Committee for determining the people we featured. Having to limit the number, we honored the defensive players they selected as Athletic Hall of Fame inductees.

We express our thanks and appreciation to Doug Mannheimer for his passion and care of the Sod Cemetery and for managing the tradition with the home game Sod Talks. This is a great tradition and he makes it special!

We are grateful to Judge Jim Joanos for his advice, input, coaching and encouragement — he was with us from the start. He inspired us and helped with the Harbison chapter. His passion for FSU is contagious! Only his wife, Betty Lou, knows more facts about FSU sports.

We are grateful for the historic work of Dr. James Jones' — "FSU One Time" and Bill McGrotha's — "First Forty Years of FSU Football." Their documentation of FSU football history helped us check our facts and keep our story straight.

Thanks to Atlantic Publishing Team, but to especially Danielle Lieneman for her talent and skills — a true professional! She was able to deal with our limited computer skills and still get the job done. Even though she is a University of Florida graduate, she supported our theme and story. A real pro!

We would like to thank Cristy Crawford and Hailey Wallace, for clerical help in formatting and editing our original manuscript, plus assisting us with graphic art concepts and designs.

We want to thank our wives and best friends, Betty and Nell for their encouragement, proof reading, recommendations for better ways to express our thoughts, and for their patience with two jocks with limited computer and writing skills. We believe if you can't spell a word at least three ways, you aren't creative. However, they knew better and kept us on track. Betty and Nell are special!

Finally, we appreciate the Seminole celebrities that reviewed and endorsed the book: Bobby Bowden, Gene Deckerhoff, Lee Corso, Charlie Barnes, and Judge Jim Joanos.

As is the case with anything worthwhile, this was a team effort!

– John Crowe and Dale McCullers: Teammates and Brothers!

WORKS CITED

DEDICATION - JOHNNY P. STEPHENS JR.

Joanos, Jim. "An American Hero….Johnnie P. Stephens." *Garnet and Old,* December 2003.

COACHES COMMENTS

Bowden, Bobby. Personal Interview. 22 May 2018.

Wyant, Gary. Personal interview. 28 April 2018.

CHAPTER 3

"Lee Corso." FSU Athletic Hall of Fame Committee. 1978. www.nolefan.org/football/corso_lee.html.

CHAPTER 4

Hogan, Pat. "Florida State Football Handbook." 1958.

McEwen, Tom. "The Morning After: Romeo kept preaching until the end." *Tampa Tribune,* 8 May 1996.

"Tony Romeo." FSU Athletic Hall of Fame Committee. 1988. www.nolefan.org/football/romeo_tony.html.

CHAPTER 5

"Bud Whitehead." FSU Athletic Hall of Fame Committe. 1981.
  http://www.nolefan.org/football/whitehead_bud.html.

Whitehead, Bud. Personal interview. 24 March 2018.

CHAPTER 6

"Gene McDowell." FSU Athletic Hall of Fame Committee. 1985.
  www.nolefan.org/football/mcdowell_gene.html.

Green, Shannon. "UCF Embraces Former Head Coach Gene
  McDowell." *Orlando Sentinel*, 18 September 2015.

McDowell, Gene. Personal interview. 10 April 2018.

Sammons, Michael. "The Experimental Kid." 2000.

CHAPTER 7

"Dick Herman." FSU Athletic Hall of Fame Committee. 1985.
  www.nolefan.org/football/hermann_dick.html.

CHAPTER 8

"Jack Shinholser." FSU Athletic Hall of Fame Committee. 2007.
  www.nolefan.org/football/shinholser_jack.html

CHAPTER 9

"Winfred Bailey." FSU Athletic Hall of Fame Committee. 1989.
  www.nolefan.org/football/bailey_winfred.html.

Bailey, Winfred. Personal interview. 10 May 2018.

Jones, Dr. James. "FSU One Time." 1973.

CHAPTER 10

"John Crowe." FSU Athletic Hall of Fame Committee. 1991.
  www.nolefan.org/football/crowe_john.html.

CHAPTER 11

"Walt Sumner." FSU Athletic Hall of Fame Committee. 1982. www.nolefan.org/football/sumner_walt.html.

CHAPTER 12

"Dale McCullers." FSU Athletic Hall of Fame Committee. 1984. www.nolefan.org/football/mccullers_dale.html.

CHAPTER 13

"T.K. Wetherell." FSU Athletic Hall of Fame Committee. 1991. www.nolefan.org/football/wetherell_tk.html.

Wetherell, T.K. Personal interview. 15 March 2018.

CHAPTER 14

Harbison, Bob. "FSU Football Playbook. " 1960.

Joanos, Jim. "A look back at a legend, Harbie." *Garnet and Old.*, September 2006.

CHAPTER 17

"J.T. Thomas." FSU Athletic Hall of Fame Committee. 1979. www.nolefan.org/football/thomas_jt.html.

Thomas, J.T. Personal interview. 22 August 2018.

CHAPTER 15

Jackson, Bobby. Personal interview. 15 March 2018.

CHAPTER 16

Wyant, Gary. Personal interview. 28 April 2018.

CHAPTER 18

Joanos, Jim. "Remembering Bill Peterson." *Garnet and Old*, May 2010.

CHAPTER 19

Andrews, Mickey. Personal interview. 26 May 2018.

"Bobby Bowden. FSU Athletic Hall of Fame Committee. 2012. www.nolefan.org/hof/bowden_bobby.html.

Bowden, Bobby. Personal interview. 22 May 2018.

Gladden, Jim. Personal interview. 25 May 2018.

"Jim Gladden." FSU Athletic Hall of Fame Committee. 2018. www.nolefan.org/hof/gladden_jim.html.

"Mickey Andrews." FSU Athletic Hall of Fame Committee. 2010. www.nolefan.org/hof/andrews_mickey.html.

CHAPTER 22

McGrotha, Bill. *1967 Year in Review, Tallahassee Democrat,* 16 September 1967, page 9.

McGrotha, Bill. *1967 Year in Review, Tallahassee Democrat,* 24 September 1967, page 1C.

CHAPTER 23

McGrotha, Bill. *1968 Year in Review, Tallahassee Democrat,* 9 September 1968, page 1C.

CHAPTER 24

"The Holy Bible." King James Version. Christianity Today, Inc. Washington D.C. 1965. Produced by The Iversen Associates. New York, N.Y. 1963

About the Authors

JOHN CROWE

John graduated from FSU in the spring of 1969 and received a regular commission in the USAF. John completed his master's degree in mathematics at FSU before going on active duty in 1971. He had overlapping careers with 26 years of military service and 33 years in the forest products industry. John retired from the military in 1997 as a Lt. Colonel, a senior pilot, and a Vietnam veteran. In 2013, he retired as the Chairman of the Board and CEO of Buckeye Technologies, Inc. John now splits time between his homes in Tallahassee, Florida and Lake Toxaway, North Carolina. He enjoys the outdoors, especially hiking, fishing, and hunting. He and his wife, Betty, enjoy traveling. Betty is also an FSU graduate from the spring of 1969.

DALE MCCULLERS

After graduating from FSU in the spring of 1969 with a criminology degree, Dale was drafted by the Miami Dolphins in the summer of 1969. He later joined the Baltimore Colts for two seasons (1970-1971) and was a member of the 1970 World Champion Baltimore Colts (Super Bowl V) team. Dale then pursued a career in law enforcement, which culminated in a 23-year career as a special agent of the Naval Criminal Investigative Service (NCIS) in various assignments throughout the world. Dale now lives in Waycross, Georgia, where he farms, writes, and spends quality time with his family in between traveling.